UNFINISHED BUSINESS
REFORMING THE HOUSE OF LORDS

Ivor Richard (Lord Richard QC) was Labour Leader in
the Lords, 1992–8, latterly in Tony Blair's cabinet as
Lord Privy Seal and Leader of the House. In that
capacity he was lead minister on Lords reform. He was
EC Commissioner for Social Policy, 1981–4; UK
Ambassador to the United Nations, 1974–9; a junior
defence minister, 1969–70 and MP for Baron's Court,
1964–74.

Damien Welfare was Special Adviser, Lord Privy Seal,
1997–8, and was previously Assistant Secretary (Parliamentary and European Affairs) at the Association of
Metropolitan Authorities. He has specialised in parliamentary matters and the House of Lords, mostly on
behalf of local government, since the mid-1980s.

Ivor Richard and Damien Welfare

UNFINISHED BUSINESS

Reforming the House of Lords

VINTAGE

Published by Vintage 1999

2 4 6 8 10 9 7 5 3 1

First published in Great Britain by
Vintage 1999

Vintage
Random House, 20 Vauxhall Bridge Road, London SW1V 2SA

Random House Australia (Pty) Limited
20 Alfred Street, Milsons Point, Sydney,
New South Wales 2061, Australia

Random House New Zealand Limited
18 Poland Road, Glenfield,
Auckland 10, New Zealand

Random House South Africa (Pty) Limited
Endulini, 5A Jubilee Road, Parktown 2193, South Africa

Random House UK Limited Reg. No. 954009

A CIP catalogue record for this book
is available from the British Library

ISBN 0099289598

Papers used by Random House UK Ltd are natural, recyclable
products made from wood grown in sustainable forests. The
manufacturing processes conform to the environmental
regulations of the country of origin

Set in 10½/12 Sabon by SX Composing DTP, Rayleigh, Essex
Printed and bound in Great Britain by
Cox & Wyman, Reading, Berkshire

CONTENTS

Part Two: Moving to Reform

Chapter 3. The Government's Approach

Chapter 4. The Key Choice

Chapter 5. A Full Reform Package

Conclusions and Summary

ACKNOWLEDGEMENTS

This book has been written quickly and amidst events as they have developed. We are very grateful to a number of people who have given valuable assistance and responded to requests for information, often at short notice. We express our thanks to them all, including: Lynn Gardner; David Jones, Librarian, House of Lords, and his colleagues; Janet Jones; Mary Morgan and her colleagues in the House of Lords Information Office; Marianne Morris; and Greg Power, Acting Director, Charter 88. Other members of our families, friends and colleagues, particularly Kathy Sutton, have been enormously encouraging both at the outset and during the course of the project. For their enthusiasm and advice we are deeply grateful.

We acknowledge a debt to Professor Robert Hazell and The Constitution Unit, whose pioneering work in this field has been a major contribution to constitutional reform.

Particular thanks are due to Will Sulkin, Jörg Hensgen and their colleagues at Vintage, who have been unfailing in their enthusiasm and patience, and to the copy editor, Katherine Fry. They have produced the book at record speed.

Errors and omissions are, of course, our own.

Ivor Richard
Damien Welfare
London, February 1999

PART ONE

FRAMING THE ISSUES

INTRODUCTION

Further reform of the House of Lords is now unfinished business as the 20th century reaches its end.[1]
White Paper on Lords reform

LORDS REFORM IS unfinished business from 1911. Since then, governments of all political colours have left the riddle unanswered. Now Tony Blair's Government is trying again.

In the past, the issues have been fought out above the heads of the voters. Should the second chamber be elected? What should it do? What should be the proper balance between the Commons and Lords? The debates in 1911, 1948 and 1968 were treated as matters primarily for parliamentarians. Yet now the questions are starting to come before the electorate. A Royal Commission is to report after wide public consultation. There may be a referendum, possibly linked to the decision on voting reform for the Commons. Detailed proposals for reform may appear in party manifestos for the general election due in 2001/2.

The bill to remove hereditary peers from the second chamber is important. But intellectually it is the easy part. The central issue is not whether hereditary peers should go. Even leading Conservatives now concede that there is no longer any rational basis on which legislators should be chosen by birth. The key question is what should take their place; and, for many people, whether at least the overall shape of an

3

eventually reformed House should be known before they are replaced. The general public needs to know more about Lords reform so that it can exercise a proper choice in answering this vitally important question. The issue goes to the heart of the strength of our parliamentary system and the quality of government it produces.

In this book, we have aimed to present the issues for the ordinary voter; we have tried to be fair but, of course, we have a point of view. In the final chapter, we argue that the best option would be a second chamber which is two-thirds elected and one-third appointed, the appointed members being independents. We are not alone in taking this view; across the political spectrum there is growing support for this option. It has, moreover, a cross-party lineage. As long ago as 1978, a Conservative committee chaired by the late Lord Home of the Hirsel recommended a model along these lines. But we discuss all the options so that the reader can make his or her own decision.

Chapter One looks at the role and composition of the present House and at the history of reform. Chapter Two sets out the case for the Labour Government's reforms and looks at how effectively the present House works as a revising chamber. Chapter Three examines the Government's approach in its White Paper, the different options for reform and the task of the Royal Commission. Chapter Four looks at the central choices behind the different types of membership. The final chapter sets out a plan for a wholly reformed House, its place in the constitutional and parliamentary structure and what it should do. The Conclusion includes a summary.

The Government's policy

The Government's policy on Lords reform was set out in its manifesto in 1997:

> As an initial self-contained reform, not dependent on further reform in the future, the right of hereditary peers to sit and vote in the House of Lords will be ended by statute. This will be the first stage in a process of reform to make

the House of Lords more democratic and representative. The legislative powers of the House of Lords will remain unaltered.

The system of appointment of life peers to the House of Lords will be reviewed. Our objective will be to ensure that over time party appointees as life peers more accurately reflect the proportion of votes cast at the previous general election. We are committed to maintaining an independent crossbench presence of life peers. No one political party should seek a majority in the House of Lords.

A committee of both Houses of Parliament will be appointed to undertake a wide-ranging review of possible further change and then to bring forward proposals for reform.

These words will doubtless be picked over exhaustively in the debate. They represent both what the Government has promised to do, and what, under the 'Salisbury Doctrine' (the convention that manifesto commitments are not opposed[2]), the Lords should sooner or later allow to pass without forcing the Commons to override them.

As the manifesto says, the Government has a two-stage policy, the first stage being the removal of the sitting and voting rights of hereditary peers. Critics say that there will be no second stage. The Government, they claim, will have no incentive to move beyond a nominated House, dubbed 'the biggest quango in the land'. They argue that the Government should reveal its plans before hereditary peers are replaced by a House of patronage. The Government rejects this, stating that the 'transitional' House of life peers will be temporary. It has, however, produced no blueprint for eventual reform nor a timetable. Instead, it was announced in October 1998 that a Royal Commission is to examine the issues for 'stage two'. It will report by 31 December 1999. A White Paper was published on 20 January 1999, setting out a number of issues for the Royal Commission.

The Royal Commission was an important change to the manifesto proposal for a joint committee of MPs and peers, since it made the inquiry independent and open to the public rather than one confined to politicians. Ivor Richard had always supported this but persuading his colleagues of it was a gradual process. It also avoided the charge that a government with a large majority might be tempted to influence the joint committee's findings. The Government still plans, however, to have a joint committee, after the Royal Commission has reported, to examine what the White Paper calls the 'parliamentary aspects' of reform.

Significantly, the manifesto does not actually commit the Government to undertake a second stage of reform; only that the joint committee (which is a parliamentary body, not part of the Government) would review 'possible' further change and bring forward its proposals. In a Lords debate on reform the Leader of the House, Lady Jay, went a little further but still avoided an outright commitment:

> We must 'get on with it' to achieve an improved transitional Chamber of appointed Peers, and then develop an appropriate second Chamber for the next century.[3]

These carefully chosen words still left it open to sceptics to query how much an 'appropriate' chamber might differ from the 'transitional' one produced by removing hereditary peers.

Tony Blair had already confronted these doubts in terms which should have confounded his critics. On the Radio 4 *Today* programme, he said:

> There are two stages to the reform: one is getting rid of the position of the hereditary peers, and secondly there is the longer-term reform for a more democratically elected second chamber. I think it is important that we do both things.[4]

He seemed to settle the argument by making clear his commitment both to a second stage and to a House with a 'democratically elected' element. Frustratingly, however, the Government has not always helped its own case on Lords reform. His statement was not taken up by other ministers and most journalists missed it. The Opposition were allowed to ignore it, preferring to repeat their charge that there will never be a second stage. Three months later, in the debate, Lady Jay's formulation was rather different. She and other ministers were offered an opportunity to endorse the Prime Minister's statement but did not do so.

Both the substance and timing of reform remain to be clarified. Having decided to hold a Royal Commission, the Government has understandably not wished to pre-empt it by announcing detailed proposals of its own. Equally, so long as it does not indicate a firm preference of its own, it remains vulnerable to its critics. The Government has said that it will not give evidence to the Royal Commission (though the Labour Party will), but it will need to adopt a clearer policy approach at some stage.

As to timing, Tony Blair and Paddy Ashdown have both hinted that the referendum on voting reform for the Commons could also cover reform of the Lords.[5] If the two issues are to be linked in this way, the objective should be to drive each forward rather than hold either back, as a leading article in *The Times* implied. A joint referendum could be used by opponents of either Commons or Lords reform to cancel out the other – or even both. Opponents of the Jenkins proposals on electoral reform have searched for delaying tactics. They argue that a referendum before the next election would prejudice the system for that contest, and then point to a boundary revision due in the next parliament as a reason for further delay after that. If no decision on Lords reform were to be taken until a referendum in the next parliament, the prospects for legislation in Tony Blair's second term could become remote. On the other hand, the Royal Commission is due to report in 1999, in time for the Government to legislate in this parliament or for it and other parties to seek a mandate for their proposals at an election in 2001/2. It has been suggested that the element of overlap between the two decisions is largely one of voting systems (if one is needed for the second chamber) on the assumption that they might be different. In the case of the second chamber, the prior questions of its composition, role and powers are more important and have no connection with the voting system for the Commons. While it might make sense to dovetail approaches to voting systems in some way, even this need not require simultaneous decisions.

The effect of the Cranborne/Weatherill agreement

Viscount Cranborne's deal over Lords reform moved the debate decisively on to what should form the second stage, the fully reformed House. It succeeded in preserving 91 hereditary peers until stage two comes into being. On the night of the announcement, Lady Jay said that stage two could follow before the next election.[6] Within days, Downing Street was telling the press the same thing: if the deal was adhered to, the Royal Commission would report in time for legislation on the second stage to go through before – rather than after – the next general election.[7]

The reason was that the deal encompassed stages one and two. Whereas the Labour manifesto said that reform would take place in two independent stages, the deal linked them. It was not just that the presence of the 'hereditary hostages' would be a continuing reminder of unfinished business. The crucial point was that for Labour now to fulfil its manifesto pledge by the next election to remove the hereditary peers, it had to introduce stage two within this parliament. If that timetable proved impracticable, to avoid the charge that it had failed to carry out its promises it would at least need to go into the next general election with a clear manifesto commitment to introduce stage two in its second term.

The initial reaction of the Conservatives in the Commons was anger. They could not accept that the situation had been transformed along the lines they had been seeking. Their spokespeople, led by Liam Fox MP, continued to claim that the Government had no intention of moving to stage two. Andrew Tyrie MP, from the backbenches, wrote two weeks afterwards in *The Times* that Lord Cranborne had been 'sold a pup' by Labour. Downing Street, he said, still wanted a nominated House. If that could not be achieved, 'the Prime Minister would only permit a fully reformed chamber in which he could control the membership, whether elected or not'. How would this be done? 'Blair will want to vet appointments with an electoral college or a closed list for any elected element.'

Some others preferred to see the deal as pointing to a Government intention to achieve a permanent nominated House by simply letting the 91 hereditary peers stay until they died. Others again discounted the view that the Government was necessarily committed to stage two on a faster timetable. Labour, it was argued, had always promised informally to offer life peerages to a few hereditary peers. The deal merely achieved this in a different way.

The underlying political realities, however, are twofold. First, the argument has moved on and public expectations of a speedy and complete reform have been significantly raised. Second, the Conservative Party has its own reasons for presenting the issue of the Cranborne deal in the way it did. It knows, as does the Government, that if for any reason stage two were still not to happen, or were to be delayed beyond the timetable which the public have now been led to expect, they would have a political opportunity to put forward a reform scheme of their own and thus outflank the Government.

Moving ahead

There should be no lack of political will on the part of the Government. The textbooks assert that governments do not give away power but this one has already proved them wrong. New Labour was elected on a programme of pluralist politics and devolution. Its constitutional programme is delivering the largest handover of power in generations – to Scotland and Wales, to the regions, to local government and to the citizen in the form of human rights and the choice as to electoral reform. Now it is the turn of parliament to be strengthened. In recent generations, the Lords' lack of legitimacy has prevented the House from using most of its powers. Opponents of reform claim that a chamber of appointed peers will be more compliant than the present House. But if, as the Government believes, life peers are more legitimate than hereditary peers, it follows that even stage one alone will produce a second chamber which is more troublesome to the government of the day. In those circumstances – and this is important to MPs – the issue is not whether there should be a stronger counterweight than at present to the House of Commons, but what form it should take.

The Lords and Commons each have a role to play in delivering reform. In the Lords itself, the Opposition under Lord Strathclyde need to recognise their responsibilities – as they failed to do in 1998 when Ivor Richard opened talks to see whether an agreed reform was possible. In the past, Conservative leaders have conceded the case for reform. As overwhelmingly the largest political group, they should now give a lead to hereditary peers as a whole and cooperate in reform rather than obstruct it.

The last attempt at reform, in 1968–9, was destroyed by Michael Foot and Enoch Powell's filibuster in the Commons. Foot felt nothing should be done to weaken the hegemony of the House of Commons. This time, opponents of reform may try to conjure similar fears among MPs about a second stage. Much has changed, however, in the last thirty years. It is simplistic to argue today that the interests of democracy only demand that the House of Commons be supreme. It was the House of Lords – however much against the odds – which provided in the 1980s and 1990s some measure of balance to ideological government. In the face of the massive majorities of 1983–7 and 1987–92, Opposition MPs could do nothing except put the arguments. In Chapter Two we set out a roll-call of small and medium-sized improvements and changes wrought to government bills by the Lords which, while not stopping measures such as the poll tax, demonstrated repeatedly the value of a second chamber in a period of polarised party politics.

Globalisation and the European Union, moreover, have shown the limits of sovereignty within one country. Power no longer comes solely from a parliamentary majority; solving political problems requires the mobilisation of mass consent as well. The experience of Thatcherism has changed British politics, driving the left to reject the politics of hegemony and winner-takes-all in favour of individual rights and checks and balances in the interests of good government. New Labour has championed inclusiveness, decentralisation and a willingness to work across traditional political, industrial and social boundaries in the search for pragmatic solutions. Reform of the Lords offers another way to diversify and strengthen our democracy.

Many Labour MPs who were elected in May 1997 are in highly marginal seats. For them, Lords reform may offer the opportunity – perhaps the best they will encounter – to make their mark on something historic. Those interested in constitutional reform will have the chance to speak out for a reform which, as we argue later, will ultimately strengthen the Commons as well as the Lords. If MPs are willing to move beyond tribal politics, they can both give themselves a crucial voice in the debate and enable Tony Blair to be bold.

There is every reason to be confident that he will be. Chances to reform our constitution come only rarely. Lords reform is big politics; it is easily the most important item in the Government's constitutional programme apart, possibly, from devolution to Scotland. The Prime Minister should ignore advice that banishing hereditary peers is enough. There is a larger game to be played. If Tony Blair produces a Lords reform which is durable and respected, he will have succeeded where every previous reforming administration this century has failed or left the job unfinished. We hope that he will do so. As he knows, statesmanship is also good politics.

CHAPTER ONE

THE PRESENT HOUSE OF LORDS

To understand how to reform the Lords, one needs to know precisely what it is and what it does. This chapter attempts to answer those points.

The House of Lords is the largest second chamber in the world and will remain so after the removal of hereditary peers.

Hereditary peers are those who have inherited a title which confers the right to sit in the second chamber of parliament. The United Kingdom is the only developed country in the world which still accords representation to an aristocracy. Alongside them, since 1958, have sat life peers, people who have been elevated to the peerage for their own lifetime and whose title and right to sit in the Lords dies with them.

The membership of the Lords

The membership changes constantly, as can only be expected of a body whose members (except bishops) sit for life and which new peers who inherit seats may join at any time. At the beginning of each month the House of Lords Information Office issues an analysis of the composition. On 4 January 1999, the membership by party was:

Party	Life peers	Hereditary peers		Lords spiritual	Total
		of first creation	by succession	(bishops)	
Conservative	172	4	300	–	476
Labour	157	1	17	–	175
Liberal Democrat	45	–	24	–	69
Crossbench	119	4	198	–	321
Other	10	–	88	26	124
	503	9	627	26	1165

These figures are for the *eligible* House, i.e., they exclude peers without a writ of summons – for example, minors or those who have not applied to take up their membership of the House (67) – or those who do not expect to attend at a particular time and have taken leave of absence (63). The total membership was 1295. Ninety-one new life peers were created in the financial year 1997–8, the largest number in one year since the Life Peerages Act 1958. The proportion of the total membership who were hereditary peers fell accordingly from 70 per cent to 63 per cent.

To an observer from four decades ago, the most surprising change would be the number of life peers, who now form 44 per cent of the eligible House. Most of the Labour Party and two-thirds of the Liberal Democrats are life peers. There are 129 life peers, or 11 per cent of the eligible total, who belong to no party (i.e., they are Crossbench or Other). The existence and number of life peers is now one of the more obvious features of the House.

However, the single most obvious fact is the enormous predominance of Conservative peers. As a bald percentage of the eligible House, Conservative peers form 41 per cent while Crossbench and Other peers (excluding bishops and law lords) total 34 per cent. Labour have 15 per cent and the Liberal Democrats 6 per cent. These figures give no real picture of the political balance of the House, however, since membership of the Lords is not a job and so most members do not attend at any given time; the average daily attendance in June 1998 stood at 412 (though this figure is steadily rising).

In practice, the Conservatives have or can organise a working majority on almost any occasion they wish since enough of their peers are likely to attend to outvote the rest. Even without hereditary peers, the Conservatives would still be the largest party if no new life peers were created.

The 'Crossbenchers' are those peers who are independent of a party but who organise themselves in a loose grouping to exchange information on forthcoming business and matters of common interest. They elect a convenor to represent their interests. (The name Crossbencher comes from the benches in the middle of the chamber.) Not all independent peers choose to join the Crossbenches. 'Other' peers are outside that group and do not receive the weekly business note sent by the Crossbench convenor. This category includes the 26 Lords Spiritual: the Archbishops of Canterbury and York and 24 diocesan bishops of the Church of England. The Lords Spiritual have always been members of the House and are the only current 'ex officio' members since they hold their seats until they retire. (On retirement, archbishops are normally offered life peerages.) The law lords sit on the Crossbenches.

Crossbench and Other peers include both some of the most and least committed members. Overall, they attend least frequently: among life peers perhaps because they have busy professional lives or are long retired; among hereditary peers presumably because there is no party spur to attend and, in some cases, little interest. Many of those who are life peers will have received their peerage as an honour with no expectation to attend, and would only wish to do so when a subject of special interest to them is under debate.

Perhaps their most important feature is their unpredictability. They are, by definition, never whipped and therefore bring an element of non-party capriciousness to the proceedings. They also make it more difficult for the party managers. If they turned up all the time, business would be impossible to plan. Fortunately, they do not.

Hereditary peers of first creation are those whose hereditary peerage is held by the person to whom it was first awarded; most were created before the advent of life peerages (Lord Longford is perhaps the best known). Mrs Thatcher

14

decided to award hereditary peerages in just two cases: William Whitelaw, who as Viscount Whitelaw became Leader of the House; and George Thomas, the former Speaker of the House of Commons, who became Viscount Tonypandy. Four royal peers are of first creation (The Duke of Edinburgh, the Prince of Wales, the Duke of York, the Earl of Snowdon) and two other members of the royal family (the Duke of Kent, the Duke of Gloucester) are hereditary peers.

By type of peer, the figures for the whole House (i.e., including those without a writ of summons or on leave of absence) break down as follows:

Hereditary peers (by succession)	750
Hereditary peers (of first creation)	9
Archbishops and bishops	26
Life peers under Appellate Jurisdiction Act 1976 (i.e., 12 law lords plus retired law lords)	28
Life peers under Life Peerages Act 1958	482
Total	1295

Under the Government's stage one proposals, most of the 750 hereditary peers by succession and nine hereditary peers of first creation will lose their right to sit and vote (although six of the latter, including the Earl of Snowdon, have been offered life peerages. The other members of the royal family will leave the House). The other 536 members (life peers, bishops/archbishops and law lords) would remain members of the transitional House. Under the terms of the deal negotiated with Lord Cranborne, an amendment to the bill likely to be moved from the Crossbenches will mean that 91 hereditary peers will stay in the House until a fully reformed second chamber is introduced.

But again, bald statistics do not reveal the whole story. Division figures may give a somewhat more accurate picture of the actual shape of the House. The highest recorded attendance for a division was in 1993 on the Maastricht Treaty when 621 peers voted on whether to hold a referendum. In 1971, 509 peers voted on a motion on entry to the Common

Market (in a smaller House than today). In the key division on the poll tax in 1988, 500 peers voted; on a reasoned amendment to the second reading of the paving bill to abolish the Greater London Council (GLC) and metropolitan counties in 1984, 455 peers were in the lobbies. Such figures, however, omit abstainers or those present other than during the vote itself.

Attendance levels are affected by the time of day. The House is generally full at the beginning of the afternoon for questions. Some peers drift away during the afternoon, although another group – notably Conservative peers working in the City – arrives for the evening shift from about 5.30 p.m. Unless the whips expect a major division, the House can be fairly quiet later in the evening, although this is hardly surprising for a body whose unpaid members are mainly elderly or employed elsewhere.

A better measure of numbers is the 'working House', taken to refer to those peers who attend a third or more of sittings, though presence for any part of a day counts as attendance. In 1996/7, for example, attendance measured in the previous session would have produced a working House almost two-thirds smaller (431 peers out of 1177 eligible, excluding bishops), of whom 208 would have been hereditary and just over half Conservative. The Crossbenches would have shrunk to 90 (just 35 of whom would have been life peers) plus three life peers from the 'Other' group, not counting bishops. These are more realistic figures which perhaps reveal the true scale of the regular non-party presence. Among life peers as a whole, only 223 would have been in the working House.

One further feature which lies behind the simple statistics is the age profile of the House. On average (at least until recently) life peers have been older than hereditary peers, since by definition the latter include younger recruits. In December 1997, for example, the average age of life peers eligible to attend was 69 years, while of hereditary peers by succession it was 62 years and across the House as a whole it was 65 years. Labour has been the oldest group overall, with an average age of 67 years in December 1997, even after the first round of creations by Tony Blair following the general election. A large number of Labour peers are either too elderly or too unwell to attend regularly, if at all. At the end of 1997, 68 of Labour's then total of 158 peers were aged over 70 (and 40 of those were aged over 75). The position of Labour has been eased somewhat by a further batch of younger peers recruited in 1998, but the Government's voting weakness remains an issue.

A *product of history*

The present House of Lords is a product of history, largely a survival from the medieval and pre-industrial eras. Before the coming of democracy, the second chamber comprised the aristocrats, or those owning property. It was a fact of political life that the monarch needed to accommodate them; they were his main source of revenue and military strength and their acquiescence was essential to stable government. One of the arguments sometimes heard for the retention of hereditary peers in the second chamber is that they somehow impart to parliament a special kind of wisdom. Yet it is often overlooked by those who seek to retain them that their forebears were summoned to Westminster not for the quality of their advice but because of their power.

The rationale for a House of peers in the traditional sense has long disappeared. Apologists are driven to invent what are in fact new claims for the value of hereditary legislators: that they represent a random cross-section of abilities and types; they are disinterested adjudicators of public policy; they learnt statecraft at (mostly) their father's knee; they represent rural interests. One claim now being made for hereditary peers is that they might as well be chosen by lottery, which is hardly flattering. Even if any of these claims were true, none approaches a sensible rationale for a second chamber at the onset of the third millennium.

The present membership of the House is the result of history and incremental change rather than of any conscious decision to ensure that something or somewhere is represented. In typical British fashion, its membership has been

17

adapted rather than consciously reformed. Many of its members do a good job, and are assiduous in providing a voice for particular interests or parts of the country. But however good they are, neither hereditary nor life peers represent anybody but themselves, though they may owe their presence in the Lords to government or royal patronage.

The largest adaptation was the invention of life peers, introduced by Conservative governments to stave off more radical reform. In 1958, the expressed aim was to create more Labour peers in order to make the House more legitimate. The Labour Opposition at the time were suspicious of the bill for that very reason. In the same way, law lords – the original life peers – were introduced by Disraeli in 1876 to professionalise the judicial role of the House and avoid implementing a section of Gladstone's Act of 1873 which would have ended it. Neither innovation would have happened but for the existence of an aristocratic House based on the hereditary principle which the Conservative Party wished to preserve. It is, of course, an historical irony that having been introduced as a reason to preserve hereditary peers, life peers are now being used to replace them. It is right to bring the stop-gap to an end; but it is equally important to recognise it for what it is and what it was intended to be. The Life Peerages Act admitted individuals from the political and professional classes to the House, but avoided the issue of who should really be there – and of what they should be doing.

The role of a second chamber

All large liberal democracies have second chambers. In the UK, all the political parties are agreed on the importance of a second chamber. Despite this unanimity there is, however, no agreed role for our second chamber. Or, to put it another way, we think we know what we expect the second chamber to do but we are less clear as to why. As a result, there are in practice few clear demarcation lines between the Lords and the Commons. Much of the fear that a more legitimate second chamber would threaten the pre-eminence of the Commons has lain hidden in that fact. A long-term solution to reform will inevitably raise the need for a proper definition of the respective roles and powers of the two Houses.

Other countries show a variety of patterns. There is no single blueprint which can easily be applied to the UK. In federal countries such as the USA or Germany, the second chamber is often designed to bind in the component states. As in the USA, the states will often be given equal representation in the upper house, regardless of the size of their population, to emphasise their equal stake in the federation. In non-federal states too, representation in the second chamber can be territorial – designed to represent a distinct area rather than a certain number of people. Alternatively, it can be designed to secure a voice for minority groups or to even out imbalances of population.

The 'functions' of a second chamber will generally be different from those of the first chamber, although they will include revision of legislation, scrutiny of the executive and, usually, some form of constitutional role. In their main day-to-day role of revising legislation, second chambers are generally intended to enable the first chamber to do its job more quickly and to give the executive the time and opportunity to respond, i.e., to change its mind. Crucially, second chambers are almost invariably recognised as politically weaker than the first chamber.

In the case of the House of Lords, the position – as one would expect of an old British institution – is much more complicated. The relative status of the two Houses is determined by a centuries-old convention that the Commons are superior. This convention is so deep-rooted that it is not an issue. It is backed up by more recent legislation limiting the 'powers' of the Lords. We will look at the Parliament Acts later, but the broad point is that they do not cover all situations. The result is that in some respects the Lords' powers are still theoretically equal to those of the Commons, creating the scope, at least in theory, for overlap and rivalry. Solving that issue will play an important part in achieving a stable long-term reform.

Second chambers, therefore, tend to perform the following three types of role:

- providing constitutional checks and balances in the body politic;
- scrutinising and revising legislation, usually in the expectation that they will act as some sort of brake on the politically dominant House;
- scrutinising the actions of the executive through questions, inquiries and debates.

The House of Lords undertakes these roles with two more in addition:

- investigating issues which may not be of interest to, or are perceived to be too sensitive for, the elected chamber or which do not have political priority there;
- providing a forum for debate on issues of national importance where the fate of the government will not be called into question by the result.

Formally as the same House, but in practice as a separate court, the House of Lords also exercises a judicial role as the final court of appeal for the UK (except for criminal cases in Scotland). The jurisdiction arises from parliament's status as the oldest common law court. Twelve salaried Lords of Appeal in Ordinary, generally known as the law lords, carry out the work, assisted by retired law lords. They also participate in the legislative work of the House.

In its White Paper of 1968, the then Labour Government laid stress on the 'increasing contribution' which the Lords had made in almost all of its functions. Sensibly, it said that the issues of composition and powers had 'bedevilled all discussion of its functions in recent years' but that once they had been solved the functions of the House should be 'reviewed and developed', probably by the two Houses together. The Government's 1999 White Paper lays less stress on developing the future role of the House, except possibly in the context of devolution, although it does indicate a willingness to see more select committee work and EU scrutiny.

The *constitutional* role of the House of Lords has been obscured by its history and composition. It is nonetheless important, and has three aspects. The first concerns the revision of legislation. In other countries, it is frequently expected that a second chamber should express the case for restraint and constitutional balance; indeed, that is one of their unspoken functions. The role of requiring the lower house to re-examine an issue (which falls short of using the well-known delaying power, although it may lead to it) is a constitutional one, in that it is central to the process of bicameral law-making. In the second reading debate on the paving bill to abolish the GLC and metropolitan counties in 1984, the Liberal peer, Lord Hooson, said that the place of the House was not to control the executive but occasionally to cause it to reconsider.[1] The Lords have, however, for most of this century been unable fully to undertake that role. They have (rightly) been viewed as a partisan political body because of their anachronistic and unbalanced composition – although briefly in the 1980s, their defence of local government and other causes against the Thatcher Government changed the public perception of the House's usefulness. If it could make her pause, then by definition it could not be entirely without merit.

Fears for the future of the House and its members have meant that the ultimate power in the event of disagreement to force a delay of about one year (examined below) has fallen into virtual disuse. When it was enacted in 1911, the limited delaying power was expected to be used; and it was deployed twice within its first three years. Thereafter, however, it was not used at all in the inter-war years and only once in the post-war period up to 1991.[2] By the 1960s it was considered that it could probably be used only once, after which the House could expect to face reform. For that reason, it came to be seen as reserved for matters of the greatest (i.e., constitutional) importance. Parliament as a whole functions as it has because of the reluctance of one of its Houses to use the powers it actually possesses.

The second aspect of the Lords' constitutional role is, or should be, regarded as fundamental. The House has an absolute right to vote down a bill to extend (or shorten) the life of parliament, to prevent a government from voting itself permanently into office. This is not well known, even among politicians, but is more significant than is often realised. The power is an exception to the limitations placed on the Lords in 1911, when the life of a parliament was reduced from seven to five years. Since any serious attempt to postpone or cancel a due general election could only come from the government of the day, the Lords are – at least in theory – custodians of an important constitutional principle. The life of a parliament has been extended twice since the five-year limit was introduced, in 1915 and 1940; on both occasions in wartime and with both Houses agreeing that normal electoral politics should be postponed. However far-fetched the possibility might seem in a mature democracy like our own, this longstop power to prevent a government from unilaterally extending its term of office is obviously an important one in any democratic system, and especially apt in a country with an unwritten constitution. It is one of those unseen props which underpin the system, particularly one so reliant on conventions for most of its rules.

The third aspect of the Lords' constitutional role is that they have to agree before a High Court judge or law lord can be dismissed. Again, this has proved a 'paper power'. It has never been used for an English judge and they continue to retire after a quiet word with the Lord Chancellor in appropriate cases.

In terms of activity, the *legislative* role of the House is now dominant. The Lords spend 62 per cent of their time on revising primary and secondary legislation. Much of this time (53 per cent) is spent on *public bills* (i.e., those concerning public matters introduced by the Government or by private members of either House).[3] Most of these bills are introduced by the Government and the more controversial of them start in the Commons, although the proportion of government bills introduced in the Lords is increasing as part of the perennial balancing act over parliamentary time. The result of scrutiny and revision in the Lords is generally a bill whose details have changed considerably but which is still recognisable as the document originally introduced. The House makes a very large number of amendments to bills in each session, the overwhelming majority being government amendments which are then accepted in the Commons. In the ten sessions to 1996/7, the Lords passed an average of 1870 amendments per session, with 3066 being made in the 1987/88 session when the newly re-elected Conservative Government introduced a heavy legislative programme including the poll tax and the education reform bill. Government amendments are brought forward in response either to an issue raised at an earlier stage of scrutiny or to their own internal re-examination of drafting or policy. The pace of modern law-making means that, as draftsmen will admit privately, a bill as initially presented is little more than an early draft which both they and the lead department then reconsider continually as the parliamentary debate proceeds. The aim is, however, to get it right by the time it leaves the Lords, and they usually succeed.

A further 5 per cent of the Lords' revising legislation time is devoted to debating statutory instruments (orders and regulations) under which ministers make law under powers delegated by parliament. MPs rarely find SIs interesting (understandably) and although the Lords do not debate more than a minority of those laid before parliament, they often consider them more closely than the Commons. A small proportion of the time of the House (less than 4 per cent) is spent on private bills, that is those brought on behalf of private interests, usually commercial, or individuals.

The rest of the time 'on the floor' of the House (38 per cent) is spent *scrutinising the executive* and acting as a *forum for debate* on policy. Scrutiny and deliberation take four forms, in which any peer may take part:

1. At the start of each day's business, the government can be asked up to four oral ('starred') questions for a total of half an hour. These invariably take place before a full House. Unlike the Commons, where few supplementary questions are allowed, follow-up questions are unlimited within the time limit of 30 minutes for the four questions. Also unlike the Commons, questions are not allotted to a monthly departmental day. The result is that whereas a Commons ministerial team will prepare only once every four weeks

for Question Time, often with four or even five ministers sharing the answers, a single Lords minister, possibly with the assistance of a whip, will answer across the department's brief, and in a busy area might well have to take an oral question three or four times a week. In addition, each Thursday, one 'topical' question is taken which can be asked at short notice. Plus, some 2000 written questions are asked in the Lords each year; the number has doubled since 1994.

2. Short debates (known as 'unstarred questions'). These last one or one and a half hours and provide an opportunity for a peer to raise an issue to which a government minister will reply. The Commons equivalent are adjournment debates, although MPs often use these to raise local constituency issues in which there is little general interest. The practice in the Lords is for more peers to participate in unstarred questions and for the issue to be of more general public concern. An unstarred question is asked on most sitting days, often ending the day's business. There is also an increasing practice of taking them during a dinner break in the main business. They are increasingly popular and rose to 9.3 per cent of the business in 1997, whereas in 1993–7, questions as a whole had amounted on average to 7 per cent of the House's time.

3. General debates. Most Wednesdays are set aside for general debates usually lasting five hours, introduced by the various parties or the Crossbenchers on an agreed shared basis. To increase the number of opportunities for backbenchers, one Wednesday each month, up to the spring bank holiday, is set aside for two 'short debates' chosen by backbenchers and each lasting a maximum of two and a half hours. Debates vary in their impact although they draw heavyweight input from peers and considerable briefing from interest groups in the policy community concerned. They can be influential, particularly where they raise an emerging issue, and their nature complements rather than duplicates the work of the Commons. They account for 28 per cent of the time of the House.

4. Statements. Government announcements on important or

urgent matters are made by a statement to parliament. Most statements are made in the Commons, and can be made at any time although they are usually scheduled for 3.30 p.m. (i.e., immediately after Question Time). If they are taken in the Lords, they will be repeated verbatim shortly afterwards by the relevant minister, often interrupting the main business to do so. The decision as to whether a statement made in the Commons is repeated in the Lords is in practice made by the official Opposition, statements being offered to them for possible repetition. As in the Commons, there is then a limited time for questions to be put to the minister. Overall, from 1993 to 1997, statements occupied 3 per cent of the time of the House, although as might be expected there has been an increased number of statements in 1997–8 as the Labour Government announced its priorities.

Much of the rest of the business of the House takes places 'off the floor', that is away from the chamber. This is where scrutiny and interrogation of the executive merge into *investigating issues* in the work of select committees. The chief difference from the House of Commons' powerful select committees is that whereas they shadow government departments, Lords committees are organised on cross-cutting lines. In addition, whereas Commons committees are composed of professional politicians who either have or develop a particular interest in the area concerned, Lords committees aim to recruit some of the specialist expertise in the House, especially on the Crossbenches. In the structure of their select committees, the two Houses tend to complement each other.

The Lords have organised their work around two principal investigative select committees.

The first is the European Communities Select Committee, established in 1974 to report on proposed European legislation. The terms of reference require it to make reports on those Community proposals which raise important questions of policy or principle and on other questions which the committee considers should be drawn to the attention of the House. It has six sub-committees with a total membership of over 70 peers. These are:

A Economic and Financial Affairs, Trade and External Relations
B Energy, Industry and Transport
C Environment, Public Health and Consumer Protection
D Agriculture, Fisheries and Food
E Law and Institutions (chaired by a law lord)
F Social Affairs, Education and Home Affairs

The reports produced by the sub-committees are recognised to be of a high standard; some EU observers consider that they provide the best level of scrutiny in any member state. Indeed, to have to appear in front of one is a sometimes harrowing experience. A European Commissioner may think he knows his subject, but to appear before a Lords committee on which there are two former Permanent Under-Secretaries at the Foreign Office, a clutch of former Cabinet ministers and some genuine experts in the field is to say the least 'concentrative' of the mind. It is also somewhat humbling, which again may not be wholly a bad thing. The committee has recently extended its work into the Third Pillar of justice and home affairs.

The second select committee, the Science and Technology Select Committee, was set up in 1980 with a broad brief 'to consider science and technology'. It has two sub-committees which can meet simultaneously. Over 20 peers are members, including physicists, chemists, medics, veterinary specialists and engineers as well as lay members. In 1998, its work included reports on antibiotics and the use of cannabis in medical treatment.

Ad hoc committees are also established from time to time to examine issues, deemed of sufficient interest to warrant a one-off inquiry. Recent inquiries have included medical ethics, murder and life imprisonment. An influential report on relations between central and local government paved the way for an improvement in a troubled area of policy. Again, this is a useful process. It enables parliament to look in an objective way at issues which are perhaps too difficult or sensitive politically for the Commons to be seen examining.

In 1992, the Lords established a new type of committee,

now the Delegated Powers and Deregulation Committee, to examine the powers proposed to be granted to ministers in bills coming before the House. This committee was a genuine innovation into our legislative process. It provides a degree of scrutiny which had not hitherto existed in any formalised way. It also now examines deregulation proposals. Strictly speaking, it falls within 'legislative scrutiny' rather than investigative work and is therefore examined later when we look at statutory instruments.

The powers of the House and the relationship with the Commons

The 'powers' of the House of Lords determine what it may do in relation to the House of Commons. The Labour manifesto stated that the legislative powers of the House would remain unaltered. This is now generally taken to refer only to the transitional House produced by the removal of hereditary peers, or 'stage one'. The Royal Commission was asked to look at the functions of the second chamber, which necessarily include its relationship with the House of Commons. Change to one House cannot but affect the other. A reformed House could – and probably will – use its powers more. And the issue of the powers of a second chamber is itself closely tied into its functions and how they are performed. Possible changes to powers are discussed later. For the moment, we set out the current position.

As is well known, the UK constitution is not written down in a single place. Large parts of it appear in statute (and this is increasing, for example, with the devolution and human rights legislation). The remainder is either in cases decided in the courts or in 'constitutional conventions', the practices by which politicians and public officials consider themselves to be bound at a given moment and which after a period without challenge are considered to have become conventions. They can evolve either to fill gaps left in legislation or case law, or to modify how those rules are applied in practice. In the case of the House of Lords and how it relates to the Commons, the relationship rests on a mixture of statute and convention, with the latter frequently modifying how the statute rules apply in practice.

The central point is rightly the supremacy of the House of Commons and that House is superior to the House of Lords in three specific ways:

1. The first, and most important, is governed by a convention. The Government is formed as the result of a general election to the House of Commons. It is the leader who can command a majority in the Commons who will be asked by the monarch to form a government. The relative positions of the parties in the Lords have no impact on the political colour of the government of the day and it has no need of a majority there. (The existence of this convention, of course, is one of the reasons why the permanent imbalance in favour of the Conservatives has been allowed to persist for so long.) By extension, it is now also taken to be a convention that the Prime Minister shall sit in the Commons not the Lords (although as recently as 1940, when Lord Halifax was a contender to take over from Neville Chamberlain, this was not certain). The last Prime Minister to sit in the Lords was the third Marquess of Salisbury in 1902.

2. The House of Commons alone has powers over taxation and expenditure. The Commons had claimed a 'general privilege' over the raising and spending of taxpayers' money from the 17th century and by the 19th century this was considered a convention. The action of the Lords, however, in voting down the budget of the then Chancellor, David Lloyd George, in 1909, led to the sole powers of the Commons becoming a matter of statute two years later.

3. Under statute, i.e., the Parliament Acts of 1911 and 1949, the will of the House of Commons ultimately prevails on all 'public' matters introduced in that House as primary legislation. The effects of these Acts, though known in their generality, are frequently misunderstood.

The Parliament Acts

Until 1911, the powers of the two Houses were theoretically

28

equal, with the exception of the convention preventing the Lords from initiating or amending bills granting aid or supplies or imposing taxation. The Parliament Act of that year for the first time regulated the relations between them and limited the powers of the Lords by inventing a delaying power. It was amended in 1949 and the two pieces of legislation are known jointly as 'the Parliament Acts'. The delaying power in those Acts applies only to 'public' bills, those concerning matters of general public application, which have been introduced first in the Commons.[4]

As the Parliament Act 1911 arose from a dispute about finance, it also removed the powers of the Lords over 'money bills'. This is a bill which begins its parliamentary passage in the House of Commons and which the Speaker of the Commons certifies to contain only provisions dealing with taxation, public spending or public borrowing (excluding such activity by local government or other bodies for local purposes). Under the Act, it will become law within one month of being sent to the Lords whether or not they pass it unless the Commons direct otherwise, provided that it has been sent to them at least one month before the end of the parliamentary session. No money bill has ever had to be passed under the Parliament Acts.

These rules do not mean that the Lords cannot debate a money bill, although given the history there is great caution over it. There could, however, be no repetition here of the situation in Australia in 1975, for example, where the Government fell after the upper house refused it 'supply' (finance for public spending). Usually a money bill will be considered at second reading and, exceptionally, at later stages as well. Amendments may even be passed but the Commons are under no obligation even to consider them. In 1985, an exceptional situation arose when a money bill relating to transport in London contained retrospective measures which some peers considered undesirable. A reasoned amendment[5] was put to the vote at second reading, albeit amid disagreement as to whether the debate was appropriate, and narrowly rejected by 110 votes to 91. Had it been passed, however, it need have had no effect on the bill, and the Commons could, with impunity and propriety, have disregarded it.

Until the 1911 Act, the Lords could, at least in theory, veto any bill. The Act removed this power in respect of public bills started in the Commons. Only a bill to extend the life of a parliament is exempt. Otherwise, the Acts now confer a power to delay any other public non-money bill, introduced in accordance with a timing requirement, into the following session and for at least 12 months (half the time in the original Act).

When it was first introduced, it was expected that the delaying power would be used fairly frequently. In fact, it has hardly been used at all. Five Acts of Parliament have been passed under the procedures. Two of them were in 1914, enacting Irish Home Rule (which was never implemented) and the disestablishment of the Church of Wales. The procedures were unused between the wars, and the third occasion was to pass the Parliament Act 1949, which reduced the period of delay. No further bill was passed under the Acts until 1991, after the War Crimes Bill – allowing prosecutions in this country of alleged former war criminals – was twice defeated in the Lords on amendments at second reading. The fifth occasion was to enact the European Parliamentary Elections Bill 1998, which is described in Chapter Two. In two other cases, the Trade Union and Labour Relations (Amendment) Bill 1975 and the Aircraft and Shipbuilding Industries Bill 1976, the procedures were begun but not completed after compromises were reached.

The way in which the Parliament Acts operate is important to understanding how Lords and Commons relate to each other. In the next chapter we look at some examples. As we have seen, the principle is that a bill which is passed by the Commons in two successive sessions can, if sent to the Lords at least one month before the end of each of those sessions, become law if the Lords do not agree. The Lords can 'reject' a bill by voting it down at second or third reading or by refusing to 'agree' with the Commons over an amendment. Alternatively, since there are no 'guillotines' in the Lords, they could in theory use the absence of timetable motions in the Lords to fail to complete all the bill's stages before the end of a session, though this is unlikely and filibustering would probably be seen by many peers as falling below the standards of the House. Rejection and failure to pass a bill trigger different timings under the Acts. If the Lords reject a bill in the second session, it becomes law immediately. If they simply fail to pass it, royal assent would come at the end of the session.

In either case, there must be one year between the dates on which the Commons give the bill a second reading in the first session and a third reading in the following session. The bill as reintroduced must be worded in precisely the same way as the original which the Lords rejected, although there is provision to incorporate amendments with which both Houses agree. The delay is sometimes described as a 'one-year delaying power'. While the period would often be roughly that length, it would vary with the point in a session at which a bill is introduced, the time required to debate the bill and the duration of the two parliamentary sessions. Although a session is usually a parliamentary year, there is no set length or starting point.

Disagreeing over amendments

Rejection other than by refusing a second or third reading comes about where both Houses differ over a piece of wording (however small) and each votes twice for their version of it. This works as follows. If the Commons pass a bill, they have voted once for the relevant piece of wording. If the Lords then amend that wording, each House has taken a different view on a single occasion. Once the bill returns to the Commons, if they then overturn the Lords amendment and restore the old wording, they have voted twice for their version of the wording. Returning the bill to the Lords starts the process known informally among peers as 'ping-pong'. A further decision by the Lords to 'insist' on exactly the same words as their first version would mean total rejection of the bill. It would then die. In practice, this hardly ever occurs. The government will sometimes accept the original Lords amendment before the 'ping-pong' starts, or suggest a compromise. If it does not, the Lords will usually give in at the second

31

round. However, in rare cases, if there is very strong feeling, they may try to pass an amendment other than the original one, to keep the process going while not endangering the bill, since at the point where either House passes a different form of wording from its previous one, the counting starts again. In theory, 'ping-pong' could last until the end of the session, if one side or the other were prepared repeatedly to change the wording. In practice, a compromise is usually reached even before the second round. On the other hand, while the story of the European Parliamentary Elections Bill (told in the next chapter) illustrates the process, it also underlines the case for reform by showing what can happen if that process is abused.

The procedures are usually a means to resolve disputes rather than to generate conflict. The risk of causing delay influences the second chamber towards excessive caution. Even where there is a determination to press an issue a second time, it is rarely difficult to devise a lesser amendment to avoid triggering the delaying power, and this in itself often narrows the ground of disagreement with the Commons and points to a compromise. It is rare, too, for a government to be unable to give some ground without losing any significant face. At least until recently, the likely political consequences for the House of using the delaying power have provided another disincentive.

Apart from extending the life of parliament and private bills, the limitation on the delaying power does not apply to one other category of bills, namely those starting in the Lords. In theory, the Lords retain a power of veto over their own bills. More practically, in disputes over amendments, the Commons have no power to compel the Lords to agree after a delay, since the Parliament Acts do not apply. Lords bills have tended in the past to be relatively non-controversial, although legal bills are, by tradition, introduced by the Lord Chancellor and are not always uncontentious. The effect of introducing all key bills in the Commons is that MPs are busy in the first half of a session and the Lords become stretched in the second half. In recent years, the weight of government legislation has led business managers to introduce medium- and even large-scale bills in the Lords to maximise legislative time. The Conservative Government introduced the Police and Magistrates Courts Bill 1984 in the Lords. In the 1997/8 session, the Labour Government introduced the Teaching and Higher Education Bill, the Human Rights Bill and the Crime and Disorder Bill in the Lords. There is no distinction in a government's eyes between its bills – whichever House first sees them – and one likely feature of a stage two reform will be to remove the second chamber's veto over bills first introduced there.

Thus far we have been concerned with the formal powers of the House. There are two principal ways in which convention alters the way in which these powers are used. Both are self-imposed (and self-interested) constraints under which the second chamber has voluntarily undertaken not to exercise its powers. The first is the Salisbury Doctrine, propounded in 1945 and since accepted as a convention. The second is a weaker convention governing the Lords' approach to statutory instruments.

The Salisbury Convention

Under the post-war Salisbury Doctrine, now generally recognised as a convention, the Lords have refrained from exercising the right to reject a government bill if it gives effect to a manifesto commitment. The doctrine was originally formulated to govern the behaviour of the Conservative Opposition facing the Attlee Government's dominant majority in the Commons and the paucity of Labour peers in the Lords. It evolved from working practices adopted between the Labour Leader in the Lords, Viscount Addison, and the Opposition Leader, the fifth Marquess of Salisbury. It has matured into a convention considered to govern the behaviour of the House as a whole, and has now spilt over into a firm disinclination to attempt to vote down any government bill at second reading whether or not it formed part of the government's manifesto. The convention allows a government without a Lords majority to secure its business. Indeed, it has become the main reason why what was thought to be the original purpose of the Parliament Acts – to force through bills rejected *in toto* by the Lords – has been rendered irrelevant. Like the introduction of life peerages in the following decade, the convention is an example of the skill shown by Conservative politicians in ameliorating the worst objections and avoiding confrontation with the intention of postponing Lords reform as long as possible.

In 1945, in the debate on the King's Speech, Lord Salisbury (the then Viscount Cranborne) said:

> It would be constitutionally wrong, when the country has expressed its view, for this House to oppose proposals which have been definitely put before the electorate.[6]

This convention has often been seen as applying only to the second reading of a manifesto bill and, by implication, to the motion after third reading, by which the House formally passes the bill. It applies, however, also to the passing of wrecking amendments to a manifesto bill during its various stages. Lord Carrington, the former Conservative Leader in the Lords, has written that:

> Cranborne had to allow some robust words and tactics, but still retain sufficient control to prevent the passing by the Opposition of 'wrecking' amendments – as opposed to those which could perhaps draw a good deal of the poison from a Bill without seeming to destroy it utterly. There was, of course, argument about what constituted a wrecking amendment and what did not: but, by and large, the Salisbury strategy worked and the Salisbury convention – of no wrecking amendments – was observed. To this day the convention continues . . .[7]

In a debate on Lords reform in 1998, the then Opposition Leader, Viscount Cranborne (himself the grandson of the inventor of the doctrine), was pressed by the Government as to the present Opposition's view of the convention. He confirmed that they regard it as extending to the avoidance of wrecking amendments.[8]

There is no formal definition of a wrecking amendment, although it might be taken to describe an amendment which frustrates one or more of the key purposes of a manifesto bill. This would clearly include an amendment to remove a key clause, but would it cover, for example, an amendment to delay implementation for twelve months or, in the precise context of the bill to end the rights of hereditary peers, to suspend its operation pending the report of the Royal Commission? We are in uncharted constitutional territory.

The convention amounts to a very significant limitation on the powers of the second chamber. There is an important – and very real – difference between rejecting a motion to give a bill a second reading and passing an amendment to the text of the bill at a later stage. At second reading, if the second chamber votes down the bill it is lost. At committee or report stage, in contrast, even a wrecking amendment does not cause the bill to fall immediately. As we have seen, the bill will return to the Commons at least once and probably twice before any question arises, in practice, of the bill being blocked. While passing a wrecking amendment might be intended to express political opposition to a bill, in procedural terms it does no more than put an alternative form of wording on to the table. So the effect of the full formulation would appear to be not merely to require the House to back down if its wrecking amendment has been rejected in the Commons, but to prevent it from passing such an amendment at all. It will be interesting to see during the stage one bill whether other peers agree that the convention does in fact go as far as the present Viscount Cranborne indicated.

Statutory Instruments

Secondary legislation (statutory instruments, orders and regulations) make law just as much as when parliament passes a bill, but are decided by ministers under powers delegated to them in a parent act. They are the other area in which conventions affect the way the Lords exercise their formal powers. As such, they are inevitably less prominent and less publicised than the parent act, though they sometimes can have far-reaching practical effect. Less important statutory instruments are made by ministers without being laid before parliament (although all those of a general nature will be considered by the Joint Committee on Statutory Instruments, on which both MPs and peers serve). More significant powers are granted, subject to one of two forms of scrutiny. In dealing with a 'negative' instrument, either House has the opportunity to step in within a period and prevent the action proposed. The standard period is 40 days, not counting days when either House is prorogued or not sitting for more than four days, although the instrument may come into effect during this period. For an 'affirmative' instrument, normally reserved for the most important matters, both Houses have to give their positive assent. Instruments affecting taxation or other financial matters are for the resolution of the Commons only. Hybrid instruments – those which are affirmative and would, apart from the provisions of the authorising acts, be enacted by a private or hybrid bill – are subject to a separate procedure in the Lords.

The Lords' powers over statutory instruments were not affected by the Parliament Acts, and so the second chamber theoretically retains a right to veto both negative and affirmative instruments in the same way as the House of Commons. The fact that wide powers continue to exist has not troubled successive governments since the powers are more apparent than real. By custom the Lords do not exercise them; the House does not usually vote at all on affirmative instruments and will only rarely seek to oppose directly a negative one. As far as can be ascertained, it has never voted down a negative instrument. It has only once voted down an affirmative one, concerning sanctions against Southern Rhodesia (now Zimbabwe) in 1968, a vote which caused the breakdown of the all-party approach to Lords reform under Harold Wilson's Labour Government. Since 1968, the Conservative Party has made clear that it regards itself bound by the convention and the Labour Party has consistently upheld it. The convention has been weakened in recent years, however, by the attitude of the Liberal Democrats in the Lords to negative instruments. In 1997, they attempted to annul the Social Security (Lone Parent) (Amendment) Regulations, but were defeated by Labour with Conservative support. Some leading Crossbenchers similarly oppose the convention. It is becoming more common for the Lords to divide on critical but non-fatal motions.

As a result of the Lords' attitude, there is a clear 'scrutiny gap' because the House of Commons is too busy to debate on the floor more than a tiny fraction of the instruments made each year. Although all statutory instruments are considered by the Joint Committee, its remit is to examine whether they fall properly within the powers in the parent act and whether the drafting makes sense, not the merits of the issue. The Commons have standing committees on delegated legislation, in which some SIs are debated, but even a vote against in such a committee will not kill the instrument. Very few SIs are debated on the floor of the Commons, where (at least in theory) they may be voted down. A debate usually occurs only when one of the two main Opposition parties demands it. Examples include controversial changes to lone parents' benefits or banning beef on the bone, which were approved by the Commons on a division.

Part of the problem in devising meaningful scrutiny in either House is the rule that in general statutory instruments cannot be amended, collapsing any discussion into a simple for or against. Instead, the Lords have developed their own procedures for expressing a view without exercising a veto. A separate motion may be moved calling on the government to delay or amend the statutory instrument. The instrument itself is not affected and if this 'non-fatal' motion is carried the government is not obliged to act.

In contrast to this somewhat patchy process, as we saw earlier, the Lords have established a strong role in examining primary legislation before it is agreed to see what secondary powers it proposes. Since 1992, the Lords have had procedures whereby all bills are examined for ministerial powers before the second reading. There is no equivalent scrutiny in the Commons. The powerful Delegated Powers and Deregulation Committee identifies and reports on powers which government is proposing to take under a bill. The committee was established both to improve control over the executive and to save time in debate, since bills containing many such powers could provoke lengthy discussion.

The committee is required 'to report whether the provisions of any bill inappropriately delegate legislative power, or whether they subject the exercise of legislative power to an inappropriate degree of parliamentary scrutiny'. Acting on the advice of the committee, the House decides whether the bill should be amended. In practice, the government generally accepts the wishes of the committee; otherwise, it knows that amendments to give effect to the committee's recommendations are highly likely to be passed anyway.

The committee looks in particular for so-called 'Henry VIII' powers – where ministers are empowered to amend Acts of Parliament under delegated powers – which should be a matter for primary not secondary legislation. It may recommend, for example, that a power, which the bill proposes should be subject to scrutiny under the 'negative' resolution procedure, should instead fall within the 'affirmative' procedure, meaning that a parliamentary debate will be guaranteed before the instrument comes into effect. This committee has proved extraordinarily valuable and effective. Even now governments have to take it seriously.

The position on statutory instruments will need to be considered under the second stage reform. A House with more legitimacy might not feel bound by such a weak convention, and the Liberal Democrat Party can be expected to press this issue. The House created by the removal of hereditary peers might see no reason not to exercise its powers more often. It should be remembered that the power is to veto, not to delay. In other words, while a statutory instrument which has been voted down can be reintroduced in the Commons in the hope that the Lords will approve it the second time (as happened in 1968), the Commons have no power to ensure that their view will prevail. Much of the day-to-day business of government is conducted under statutory instruments. There would be considerable theoretical scope for the second chamber to be an irritant, and possibly worse, to the government of the day.

Another issue arises from the fact that simply opposing an instrument often fails to pinpoint the precise concern, which might otherwise be soluble with a more creative system of scrutiny. It would probably be better for all concerned to examine afresh what powers a second chamber should have over statutory instruments so that it can take a proper view of them. Given the relative lack of interest in secondary legislation among MPs, there may be scope for the second chamber to develop a more specialist role in this area, following the example of the Delegated Powers Committee. We look further at these questions in Chapter Five.

Past attempts to reform the House

Since the Government is now set on reforming the second chamber, it is worthwhile examining previous efforts to do precisely that – all of which have failed to grasp the nettle in its entirety. There have been three previous government attempts in this century radically to reform the Lords, in 1910–11, 1947–9 and 1968–9. It is helpful to see these against the background of the changing positions of the two Houses over the last 150 years.

The primacy of the House of Commons was confirmed with the successive extensions of the franchise from the Great Reform Act 1832. From a position of theoretical equality with the Commons, the Lords quickly came to be seen as a revising chamber. Many had believed that reform or abolition of the House of Lords would follow in the immediate aftermath of the Act. It did not happen. In 1867, the constitutional writer Walter Bagehot described it as part of the 'dignified' aspect of the constitution, with powers to revise and possibly to delay bills but having capacity to inspire popular reverence as its chief characteristic. Relations between the two Houses remained generally calm until the 1880s. The emergence of government by party towards the end of the century was accompanied by increased tension between the two Houses and more frequent calls for reform of the Lords. It is often forgotten that the Liberal governments of the later nineteenth century faced a House with a permanent preponderance of

Conservatives, just as Labour did when it was elected in 1997. Gladstone's bill for Home Rule for Ireland, for example, was thrown out by the Lords in 1893.

Reform schemes abounded (as now). The future Prime Minister, Lord Rosebery, proposed in 1884 and again in 1888 that life peerages should be introduced and that a select committee should be appointed to consider how the efficiency of the House might be improved. A Conservative, the Earl of Dunraven, proposed a far-reaching reform bill in 1888, and in 1894 another Conservative, Lord Curzon, proposed the ending of the automatic right of hereditary peers to sit in the upper house. In 1907, after the Liberal Government experienced difficulties, a Conservative plan was put forward which took up Curzon's idea that only hereditary peers qualified by public service should be able to sit by that right alone. Other members of the upper house would be life peers or those peers elected by their colleagues. The bill was withdrawn and a select committee appointed under Rosebery. This reported, in 1908, that possession of a peerage should not of itself confer the right to sit in the Lords and recommended a House of about 400 members, of whom the largest number would be hereditary peers elected for one parliament by their colleagues, together with other hereditary peers qualified by experience and a few life peers. The Liberal majority in the Commons, however, was more concerned to remove the veto so that a radical government could pass its bills without having to call a new election.

The opportunity came with the Lords' rejection of the Lloyd George budget of 1909 by 350 votes to 75, which led to an immediate constitutional crisis. An election ensued at which the Liberals were returned, although without their former overwhelming majority. After the Lords conceded and accepted the budget, the Liberal Government pressed ahead with its proposals to cut their powers. The Government laid resolutions in the Commons setting out how the Lords' powers might be restricted and laying the basis for the later Parliament Bill. The Lords also debated and approved a number of resolutions proposing reform of their composition. A conference between the Liberals and Unionists (or

Conservatives) failed, however, to reach agreement on powers. After the second general election of 1910, the Conservative Opposition Leader in the Lords, the Marquess of Lansdowne, tabled proposals for a reformed House in an attempt to preserve the veto. The House would consist mostly of indirectly elected members. There would be 350 'Lords of Parliament' serving 12-year terms chosen by thirds in a number of categories: members elected by peers from those holding high office; those elected by MPs on a regional basis; those appointed by the government, together with bishops, law lords and members of the royal family. These proposals were withdrawn when it became clear that the Liberal Government would proceed to remove the veto anyway and that the King was prepared to create sufficient Liberal peers to ensure the bill's passage. On the composition issue, the Government's bill stated boldly in its preamble that:

it is intended to substitute for the House of Lords as it at present exists a second chamber constituted on a popular instead of hereditary basis but such substitution cannot be immediately brought into operation . . .

The Tory leadership again conceded, after the Commons threw out their amendments, which had emasculated the bill. Lansdowne and other Opposition leaders abstained, watching the vote from the Lords gallery. Three hundred of the Unionists abstained with them but 114 'Diehards' voted against. By a Government majority of only 17 for the bill, the Lords' equal status within the Westminster parliament was brought to an end.

The Act was widely regarded at the time as a temporary measure which would be improved within a short time. Asquith's Government set up a cabinet committee to examine how to pursue the promise of further reform contained in the preamble, but it never reported to the cabinet. Instead, Lloyd George's Coalition Government, dominated by Conservatives, set up an inter-party conference of both Houses under Viscount Bryce to consider the powers and composition of the second chamber and its relationship with the House of Commons. This reported in 1918, when the Government was still preoccupied with the Great War. The House of Lords, it said, should be a revising chamber. It set out four functions for the House: the examination and revision of bills brought from the Commons; the initiation of non-controversial bills; the introduction of sufficient delay (but no more) to a bill to allow the opinion of the country to be tested (especially on constitutional bills); the full discussion of large questions, especially without the constraint that the fate of the government might rest on the outcome of a division. The 1911 Act was not seen as a permanent solution (though in essence it still subsists). The House should not be a rival to the House of Commons, but should be able to produce the 'interposition of so much delay (and no more) in the passing of a Bill into law as may be needed to enable the opinion of the nation to be adequately expressed upon it'. For this purpose, it considered, but rejected, the device of referenda; instead, there should be a process of conciliation meetings between the two Houses.

As to composition, it proposed (although not unanimously) that 246 members should be indirectly elected by MPs through a regional system of proportional representation, with a further 81 members elected by a joint committee of both Houses (all 81 being hereditary peers or bishops in the first instance, with that segment gradually diminishing). Law lords would be ex officio and all other members would serve for twelve years, being chosen by thirds. No single party should dominate the House and it should contain a number of independent members. Given the date and circumstances, coming so soon after a major constitutional confrontation, the boldness of the proposed composition is striking.

It was expected that reform would follow the Bryce Commission. The King's Speech mentioned reform in 1920, 1921 and 1922, and another cabinet committee was established by the Coalition Government to consider the issue. This concluded that the Bryce proposals would be unacceptable to the Commons and to the electorate. Instead, it tabled its own proposals for a House of some 350 consisting mainly of members 'elected, either directly or indirectly from the outside', together with some hereditary peers elected from among themselves and members nominated by the Crown. The resolutions were criticised in the Lords itself for being too vague. Indeed, some of today's arguments against reform are depressingly familiar. The Conservative Government of 1924 continued to give the issue some attention and established another cabinet committee in 1925. This led, in 1927, to proposals not unlike those tabled in 1922, which were more favourably received in the Lords but drew criticism in the Commons from Labour members and some Conservatives. Thereafter, there were various private members' bills in the Lords on reform but no further government initiatives before the Second World War. One simple reason for this may be that since Labour never had a Commons majority in these years, there was little overly controversial legislation which would have excited the Lords even to use their newly limited powers and, self-evidently, no incentive for the Conservatives to reform further.

By the time Labour achieved a majority Government in 1945 its main interest, like the Liberals 40 years previously, was in securing its legislation. The Salisbury Doctrine enabled Conservative peers to adapt to the political reality of Labour's 150-seat majority in the Commons and they accepted its nationalisation and welfare reform legislation with few difficulties. In 1938, Labour had numbered only 15 in the upper house against 80 Liberals and 400 Conservatives. Attlee, the post-war Labour Prime Minister, created 44 Labour peers in his six years in office, enabling the Government to function more effectively. The fear of Conservative obstruction remained, however, and became focused on the Government's plans to nationalise the steel industry. A new parliament bill, which would cut the period of the Lords' delaying power by twelve months, was introduced in 1947.

This bill was adjourned in the Lords while a Party Leaders' Conference was convened to see whether an agreed reform could be achieved covering both composition and powers. This eventually broke down over a three-month gap between the parties in the length of the proposed delaying power and the Government proceeded with its bill. The Conference did, however, produce a joint statement listing a number of principles which, if there had been an overall consensus, would have been submitted back to the political parties for agreement. These included that the 'present right to attend and vote based solely on heredity should not by itself constitute a qualification for admission to a reformed second chamber'.

A number of minor changes arising from the Conference were introduced in the following years, including the payment of expenses. A scheme for leave of absence for peers not intending to attend the House was introduced after 60 Conservatives, who had not attended for four years, suddenly appeared to vote against the abolition of hanging in 1956. Under the Peerage Act 1963, Tony Benn won his campaign for hereditary peers to be allowed to disclaim their peerages and remain eligible for election to the House of Commons. The number exercising the right to disclaim, however, has proved much lower than expected. The same Act ended the anomaly by which women who had inherited a title were excluded.

The Macmillan Government introduced life peerages in 1958 and this has had a profound effect on the second chamber. More life peers have been created than were originally envisaged. Numbers increased, and the House became markedly busier in the 1960s, with Labour peers mounting spirited opposition to bills. The political outlook of the House also changed. Whereas in 1956 a large majority had supported hanging, by 1965 a majority of 100 opposed it. In the later 1960s, peers were active in promoting the liberalising legislation of the 'permissive era'. In the 1980s, in the same way, many peers would be vigorous in their promotion of the interests of the disabled and those with special educational needs, and in defence of local government. The House of Lords would indeed become the main focus for opposition to the Thatcher Governments in the 1980s and, for the first time in its history, become linked in the public mind with popular causes and consequently attract public support. The need for a second chamber would once again be accepted, not through an overriding need to accommodate regional differences or strengthen the political centre of the country, but because of the obvious value and importance of the work of revision and scrutiny.

Another unforeseen consequence of the Life Peerages Act was the increase in the number of Crossbench peers. While they had always existed, it had not originally been intended to include life peerages in the Honours lists. One result was that the number of peers with distinguished expertise increased and added a new factor to the possibilities for reform, to which we shall return.

A decade after the Life Peerages Act, the Wilson Government made the third attempt at reform. A cross-party committee, continuing work in the Lords, produced a fair measure of agreement. The scheme which it produced, however, was less radical than those which had been discussed in earlier years. No previous scheme had proposed a House whose sole voting members would be appointed peers. Once again, the main function of the House was seen to be that of a revising chamber, but it was accepted that the government of the day should be able to secure its bills. It was argued that the presence of hereditary peers and the large number of Conservatives weakened its legitimacy. There should continue to be Crossbenchers with expertise. Peers should be divided into voting and non-voting members and there should be a retirement age so that new peers could be created without increasing the overall size of the House.

The talks broke down when, in June 1968, Conservative peers voted down an affirmative order giving effect to sanctions against Ian Smith's rebel regime in Southern Rhodesia. The Government decided to go ahead with its own White Paper and bill, the former appearing in November 1968. The proposals, however, largely reflected the earlier cross-party talks. All hereditary peers would eventually go, although they could remain as non-voting members for their lifetime. Life peers would be voting peers, provided they attended one-third or more of sittings and were aged under 72. The bishops and law lords would remain, although in smaller numbers. The size of the voting House would be about 230. The government would be the largest party but would have no overall majority. On the functions of the House, there would be a delaying power of six months from the point of disagreement (i.e., calculated differently from the Parliament Acts but probably unlikely to reduce the actual period of delay by so much in most cases). The White Paper endorsed the Bryce list of functions and added to it the roles of looking at subordinate legislation, dealing with private bills and scrutiny of the executive. It said that the functions could at a later stage be extended and developed and it made clear that it saw the development of the functions of parliament as a whole 'as the most positive ground for reform'.

The Lords debated the White Paper and overwhelmingly endorsed it by almost five to one (250 to 56), with majorities in favour from all the groups and almost twice as many Conservatives supporting as opposing it. The Government then introduced the Parliament (No. 2) Bill into the Commons. It received a second reading but as a constitutional measure it was taken in committee of the whole House, where all MPs could take part, rather than in a standing committee. The result was that it became totally bogged down as two backbenchers from opposite ends of the political spectrum, Michael Foot and Enoch Powell, joined forces to talk it out. There were two issues: whether the second chamber should be strengthened and the extent of patronage contained in the bill. They jointly exploited a situation in which divided views among MPs (some wanting abolition, others an elected House in preference to an appointed one) were matched by only lukewarm frontbench support, notably on the Tory side. Unable to drive through a guillotine, the Government became stranded as its own popularity flagged and other priorities became more pressing in the legislative programme. The bill was withdrawn.

The fact that reform failed in the Commons, not the Lords, removed from peers for a generation a sense of responsibility, which they felt derived from their illegitimate composition. It also enabled them to lay aside some of the restraint which had characterised their behaviour in the inter- and post-war years, notably in their response to the Labour Government in the 1970s, as we shall see in the next chapter. Labour MPs who have doubts about democratic reform might bear that in mind. But it also showed that the key to a successful reform of the Lords will be to establish a modern rationale for the roles of our two chambers, the relationship between them and what they represent. Anything short of that will be another partial reform which will not be stable. A reform which achieves that, however, can see emerge not only a more legitimate second chamber, but a strengthened House of Commons as well.

CHAPTER TWO

THE CASE FOR REFORM

... the one aspect which no one can defend – the hereditary peers ...
Lord Baker of Dorking, in a debate on reform of the House, 14 October 1998[1]

KENNETH BAKER IS right. Some have tried, but none has succeeded, to provide a modern justification for the principle of heredity in parliament. Others, including the Opposition frontbench in the Lords, have not even made the attempt. Instead, they have argued about process or practicalities, not the central idea of what parliament is for or who should be in it. The debate in which Lord Baker spoke lasted for two days, yet by the end of it the case for change stood virtually unscathed.

There are three principal reasons for reforming the second chamber:

1. The rationale for hereditary peers having seats in the second chamber has long since vanished; and with it much of the legitimacy of the House.

2. The present House is politically unbalanced.

3. Its lack of legitimacy means that it cannot do its job as well as it should.

1. The rationale for hereditary peers in the second chamber has long since vanished

While in the past there was a need to accommodate landed magnates within the political (and judicial and economic) system, that need has disappeared with the coming of democracy. All countries have systems of inheritance to manage the inevitable passing on of land, possessions and money, and this is especially important where land – which is finite – is the basis of wealth. Heredity became the qualification to enter the second chamber as a by-product of the importance of land and titles, and the consequent social standing associated with it. At the end of the twentieth century, we are confronted with a system whose original purpose is no longer even a memory. The second chamber lacks parliamentary legitimacy because its core membership no longer has, as a group, any proper claim on power.

In principle as well as practice, this is an unsatisfactory situation which any reforming government ought to feel the need to address. Parliament is weakened because one of its chambers has been suspended for most of this century between past and future. No one would design its present composition from scratch. It is unable to undertake its full responsibilities through fear of the consequences. The largest legislative chamber in the world remains workable only because the majority of its members do not attend, and because it dares not exercise the powers it actually possesses. The relationship between Lords and Commons has been unsatisfactory since the last attempt at reform failed in the Commons in 1969, as the experience of not only the Wilson/Callaghan but also the Heath Government demonstrated. The fact that the Thatcher and Major Governments refused to pursue reform – despite prompts from a number of their supporters – derived directly from narrow political self-interest.

2. The present House is politically unbalanced – grotesquely so

The Conservative Party still dominates the second chamber, as it has done for more than a century. No other second

49

chamber in the world has an effective permanent majority for one party. In no other legislature does the result of a general election have no effect on the political composition of the second chamber. In no other legislature can one party expect to win most of the divisions on a permanent basis; and, moreover, in an emergency, summon additional supporters from among its infrequent attenders to make the result certain. The overwhelming majority of hereditary peers who take a party whip (88 per cent), or nearly half of the total of hereditary peers, excluding those without a writ or on leave of absence, identify themselves with the Conservative Party.[2] During the 18 years of Conservative control, the imbalance actually became worse. As Prime Minister, Mrs Thatcher created one and a half times as many Conservative life peers as Labour and Liberal Democrats combined. John Major allowed slightly increased numbers to the Opposition parties, enabling them to renew their frontbench teams, but he still created more Conservatives. It is a ludicrously inequitable position. If it were not so serious, it would indeed be laughable. In some ways it already is, as anyone who tries to explain it to a group of American students cannot fail to recognise.

The unfairness of the Conservatives' approach was outweighed only by its stupidity. Thoughtful Conservatives now blame it for the Labour Government's proposals for reform. They argue that if only Labour were not now facing a massive majority of its opponents in the second chamber, it would have been prepared to overlook reform. The Conservative historian and life peer, Lord Skidelsky, called it 'a serious rational grievance'.[3] Even the former Conservative Leader, Viscount Cranborne, has suggested that he disagreed with the approach. In fact, of course, the political imbalance against the Labour Government underlines an unfairness but is not the most important issue. The continued presence of hereditary peers in the second chamber would be inappropriate whichever party they supported.

The history of government defeats over the last 25 years shows the degree of that political imbalance. Under the Blair Government, there were 36 defeats on bills during its first session in 1997/8. These included an attempt to postpone the referendum on a mayor and assembly for London by requiring the bill creating them to be published eight weeks before the ballot (and months earlier than planned), and seeking to remove statutory restrictions on the creation of local 'assisted places schemes' for private education, when the removal of the national scheme had been a manifesto commitment. In addition to the 36 defeats on bills, there were two defeats on motions (one protesting at the banning of beef on the bone and the second a rare device criticising 'asperity of speech' in debate) and the decision of the House on a free vote to reject lowering the age of consent for homosexual men. As the Government generally made clear at the time, on all but five occasions the defeats on bills would have gone the other way if no hereditary peers had voted, as would the two motions.[4]

It is an open secret in the Lords that the Conservatives frequently avoided pressing divisions during the first session of the Blair Government to avoid handing it a propaganda victory. It is easy to see why. The former Conservative Chief Whip, Lord Denham, has claimed that in the post-war period the House would defeat the government of the day on 15–25 occasions per year. His rule of thumb underlines the unfairness because it applies only under Conservative governments.[5] Despite the Tories' alleged attempts at self-restraint, Tony Blair's Government suffered in its first session almost three times the average rate of defeats suffered by the Thatcher/Major Governments. In the 18 sessions from 1979 to 1997, the Conservatives suffered a total of 241 defeats, one hundred fewer than Labour in the five years from 1974 to 1979 and an average of only 13.4 defeats per session – against 36 for Blair.

The effect of the hereditary peers can be clearly illustrated by the figures for one session. In 1988/9, when Thatcherism was at its height, Donald Shell and David Beamish calculated that there were 172 Government victories and 12 defeats (excluding divisions where the Government took no view). If the votes of hereditary peers had been excluded, the Thatcher Government would have won only 21 divisions. There would have been 159 Government defeats and the result would have been a tie on four occasions.[6] In other words, the hereditary peers produced the Conservative Government's victories on seven out of every eight occasions in that session. Defeats as a percentage of all divisions ranged in the Thatcher/Major years from 4 per cent in 1986/7 to 16 per cent in 1990/91.

The Labour Government of the 1970s fared even worse than Tony Blair's Government has done. In 1975/6, the Wilson Government was defeated on 126 occasions; it lost fully 86 per cent of the divisions called. In 1977/8, the Callaghan Government lost 78 divisions or 81 per cent of those called. By comparison, the highest rate of defeat under the previous Conservative Government of Edward Heath had been 18 per cent in 1972/3, after two sessions (1970/71 and 1971/2) in which it was defeated in no more than 3 per cent of divisions.[7] In total, during Labour's five sessions from October 1974 to May 1979, it suffered 343 defeats in the House of Lords – an average of 68.5 per session.[8]

3. Its lack of legitimacy means that the House cannot do its job as well as it might

The primary role of the second chamber is to revise legislation, including from time to time asking the Commons to think again. This role can sometimes also have constitutional significance. The lack of legitimacy and political imbalance, however, mean that the House can only partially carry it out. Where it seeks to assert a view, the presence of hereditary peers denies it political authority. Moreover, its fixed dominance by the Conservatives frequently robs its views of political credibility.

This is particularly a problem under a Labour government (or, earlier in the century, a Liberal one). Some believe that under a Conservative government, the House shows sufficient independence to inflict occasional defeats and avert major errors of judgement. While it undoubtedly attempts to exercise that role, and has achieved important changes, whether, given the political imbalance, it is fully able to do so is open to debate. The classic example is the House's stopping of the paving bill to abolish the GLC and metropolitan counties, in the year before abolition went through, when the proposals to replace elected councillors with appointees were defeated. The opposite example is the 'failure' of the House to stop the poll tax – both are examined below in further detail. Under Labour, the imbalance has one of two consequences depending on how the dominant Opposition choose to play their hand. If, as in the 1970s, they inflict frequent defeats (and then give in after the Commons have reversed them) legislative scrutiny degenerates into an automatic routine and issues may not be properly examined. On the other hand, if, as apparently in 1997/8, the Conservatives, to an extent, ration the number of divisions they press, they are immediately allowing some non-partisan issues to go through which could legitimately have been raised; indeed, it is more likely that the issues raised will be those which it is hoped may make attractive headlines for the Conservatives rather than others which may involve more substance than resonance. And if they were to choose to stay their hand completely, the House would be neutered.

The imbalance affects peers in other parts of the House as well. To the extent that their point is more difficult to make effective in the division lobbies, because of the numbers sitting on the Conservative benches, they are at a disadvantage in carrying out their role and may even choose not to press an issue for that reason.

These constraints raise serious issues. Because of them, one House of Parliament is not wholly fulfilling its role. The conventions which prevent it from exercising its powers have arisen directly from its illegitimate composition. They have served both to compensate for it, but also to some extent to insulate it against reform. Its composition has been its bugbear: either its lack of legitimacy has prevented it from using the powers it has; or, when it has used them, its composition has necessarily become the issue. It is more than a matter of the inconvenience – or even indignity – of non-Conservative governments losing as often as they do; or of Opposition parties finding it difficult to defeat a Conservative government on other than unusual issues or at unexpected times of the evening. The imbalance heightens the politics either way.

Where a Conservative government loses, it is treated by press and government as either a humiliating defeat or a purely political manoeuvre. Where a Labour government loses, the government perceives it as an outrage. The merits of the amendment or point at issue can often be distorted or even lost in the middle of all this. The ordinary business of legislating in a two-chamber system, using occasional compromises – at least on small or medium-scale issues – to secure assent becomes over-dramatised at Westminster. In the same way, scrutiny or investigative work can, if it presents a political inconvenience to the government of the day, be dismissed – or ignored altogether – on the often unspoken ground that the make-up of the House is politically biased or illegitimate. We know of no other legislative chamber where restraint has been so elevated and regular inaction has become so politically charged.

The parliamentary system is out of balance. We now have a virtually unicameral legislature. We often fail to recognise this because it is so familiar; Bagehot almost wrote off the second chamber in the last century. Journalists routinely confuse parliament as a whole with the House of Commons. The basis of the system is the concept of parliamentary sovereignty, that parliament is all-powerful, but the weakness of the second chamber has allowed a position to develop where the House of Commons is thought to be all-powerful (rather than merely pre-eminent). In practice, party discipline makes government all-powerful and as a result any parliamentary reverse is seen as a political defeat for ministers. Yet the experience of what single-chamber government can produce should serve to warn us of the dangers; looking at what the second chamber, for all its faults, has tried on occasion to prevent should open our eyes to the advantages of a more balanced system which other countries take for granted. One beneficial consequence of Lords reform should be that scrutiny of legislation and the activities of government can proceed in circumstances which carry less of a political charge.

The use of the phrase 'single-chamber government' is deliberate. Formally and constitutionally, one should speak of 'single-chamber parliament', for the imbalance in the system is not really between the Commons and the second chamber, although MPs will be told that a strengthened House of Lords would weaken their position. The essential imbalance is between government and parliament, particularly in the House of Commons. A second chamber more able to fulfil its functions would partially redress the balance, obliging governments to think more deeply and to plan further ahead so that their proposals can withstand more searching scrutiny. In that event, the result for MPs, in government and on the backbenches, would be both a more satisfactory parliamentary process and more durable public policy-making.

Part of the challenge for reform is indeed how to strengthen both Houses of Parliament, as well as contributing to a more successful governmental process. What we should be seeking is a proper balancing of the powers of the two Houses together with a clear delineation of roles, so that their relative positions are not in doubt. The second chamber should be able to exercise its powers – possibly more limited ones than those it formally has at present – in a way which strengthens parliament as a whole.

More thoughtful hereditary peers recognise the constraints which their presence forces on the second chamber and have made clear they would welcome a long-term reform which strengthens the House. It is to the great credit of Tony Blair's Government that it has opened the way to this by proposing the removal of the hereditary peers and by making a deal with Conservative and Crossbench hereditary peers designed to achieve it.

The hereditary peerage

The three aspects just described should be sufficient to prove the case for reform, but the nature of the hereditary peerage supplies a number of others. Hereditary peers are unrepresentative of the country as a whole, or even of a significant section of it. Viscount Cranborne once breathtakingly claimed that hereditary peers were 'well on the way to becoming a cross-section of society'. The claim has not been repeated since, presumably because the opposite is actually the case. Six out of 10 hereditary peers 'claim a background in landowning'; 45 per cent of them went to Eton and only 1.4 per cent class themselves as 'workers'. Perhaps more significantly, only 16 out of the 750 hereditary peers are women,[9] and attempts to change this have been thwarted. In 1994, hereditary peers turned down a proposal from the former Labour minister, Lord Diamond, that the eldest child should inherit irrespective of whether they were a son or daughter. Furthermore, only two hereditary peers are from an ethnic minority and, while there are peers who are not well off, there cannot be many people among the poorest in society who consider that the House of Lords, however liberal-minded, represents them. While it may be simplistic to talk of issues of class, there can be little doubt that a House whose rationale is that it represents a tiny minority only perpetuates and reinforces divisions in society.

One aim of long-term reform should be to produce a House which is more responsive to public opinion. In fact, an important reason not to delay moving on from the transitional House would be to avoid a similar unrepresentativeness coming to be associated with a chamber of appointed professionals. At a time when the public lacks confidence in politicians, opening up new connections to parliament should be a priority. In that spirit, one of the most persuasive arguments for reform is that it is popular. The Labour Government has forged public support for constitutional reform and reform of the second chamber has the greatest electoral and polling support of any constitutional change across the country. At the general election of 1997, 60 per cent of those voting supported parties committed to this policy. Polls since have shown a clear majority wanting members of the second chamber to be democratically elected (e.g., ICM, *Guardian*, 9 December 1998; Gallup, *Daily Telegraph*, 8 June 1998).

Rather than assuming an open-and-shut case for reform, however, it is worth examining the excuses sometimes advanced for retaining the position of hereditary peers. Ingenious arguments are constantly being invented and elaborated, both by hereditary peers and by their apologists, although their sheer diffusion and multiplicity tend to underline the weakness of their case. There is nothing quite like self-preservation to stimulate this sort of intellectual activity. It certainly helps to concentrate the collective hereditary mind.

The Conservative high command has eschewed arguments of principle in favour of arguments about the process of reform. Indeed before the famous split in December 1998 between Conservatives in the Lords and Commons, the party leadership in both Houses had implicitly rejected the principle of hereditary peers by making clear that it was interested in reform and that its principal objection to the Government's proposals was that they were in two stages. Early in 1998, Viscount Cranborne agreed to Ivor Richard's suggestion of talks to establish where there was common ground, although after an initially promising opening it became clear that the Conservatives were not ready for serious negotiations at that point. In July 1998, however, they appointed a Constitutional Commission under the former Lord Chancellor, Lord Mackay of Clashfern, to examine options for reform. This incorporated six principles for reform. These were wholly unexceptionable.

- First, that any reformed chamber must be better at scrutin-ising and revising legislation than the present one.
- Second, that a substantial independent element must remain.
- Third, that the Prime Minister's powers of patronage must not be increased.
- Fourth, that the Members must be drawn from all parts of the United Kingdom.
- Fifth, that reform must be considered in the context of its effects on Parliament as a whole.
- Sixth, that the supreme authority of the House of Commons as the focus of democratic accountability in our country must remain intact.[10]

The Conservatives should have few grounds in the light of these principles for opposing a scheme for long-term reform which takes them fully into account. When they appeared, they afforded little comfort to hereditary peers.

Arguments in favour of hereditary peers, and against the Government's proposals, seem to fall into three types: principle, process and practice.

The hereditary principle

The passing of the historical rationale for the place of hereditary peers has obliged their remaining supporters to devise new arguments to justify their involvement. The key claim is independence. It is suggested that they are preferable to life peers because they owe their appointment to no living person. This is arguable at best: the reasons for a life peer's appointment are at least identifiable and derive (or should do) from his or her own merits. This is surely preferable to determining seats in parliament by what an ancestor achieved (or who they knew).

Another version of the argument would be that to establish a House of life peers is to swap one élite for another which is less independent because the great majority of its membership, those who take a party whip, are appointed for their politics. In other words, the argument is that hereditary peers hold their places as of right; they chose their politics, at least formally, when they entered the House and their party label was not a precondition of admission.

These arguments would, however, carry greater weight if more hereditary peers had actually chosen to support parties other than Conservative; or if there was any evidence that they were persistent rebels while life peers constantly toed the party line. In itself, it would not be an argument for retaining hereditary peers but is one against letting the Government's stage one proposals become permanent. As Ivor Richard put it recently: 'They sit independently, they weigh the arguments independently and then they independently vote Conservative.' It also ignores the position of the Crossbench and Other peers, who are individually genuinely independent.

Nor is it obvious that strong independence in the face of prevailing opinion is in all circumstances an advantage. While it may be healthy for a second chamber to stand out against prevailing fashion or ideology, it may also be important that its views are not simply immutable and that it is able to take account of public opinion and new ideas. The counterpart of independence can sometimes be remoteness. In assessing this issue, it can be difficult to avoid subjective judgements. In the case of political questions (i.e., the great majority of the important issues before the second chamber), whether or not hereditary peers can be described as independent is inextricably bound together with their political bias towards the Conservatives, since the majority of active peers by succession are supporters of that party. On issues which are not party matters, hereditary peers will tend to dampen what has become a natural liberalism in the House in the direction of more conservative views, at least on moral or social questions. For example, when the attempt to lower the homosexual age of consent to 16 was defeated in the Crime and Disorder Bill, a majority among both hereditary and life peers opposed reducing the age. However, whereas 152 hereditary peers voted against reducing the age and only 25 voted in favour of doing so, among life peers the majority against reducing it (138 votes to 97) was far less overwhelming.

To take another example from the same era, press reports before the Queen's Speech for the 1998/9 session suggested that the Government had postponed the planned repeal of section 28 of the Local Government Act 1988, which bans the promotion of homosexuality by local authorities. The reason given was that while hereditary peers remained in place its passage could not be guaranteed through the Lords.[11] This points to an interesting dual nature in the House, which has both conservative and liberal inclinations. When section 28 was debated, it was subjected to rigorous and hostile scrutiny in the Lords – to a far greater extent than in the Commons – and in consequence was shown to have a far narrower compass than Conservative ministers had sought to suggest. The revising chamber could fairly claim to have done its job on that occasion. It could, moreover, be argued that those of its members who took up the issue showed a stronger concern for civil liberties than their Commons colleagues. On that basis (perish the thought!), the reported reason for delaying repeal of this measure might appear to be an excuse to disguise a lukewarm commitment. Yet, considering the age of consent vote, ministers' apparent fears may be based on the likely antipathy towards repeal among the silent majority of peers, predominantly hereditary ones. Their votes in the lobbies tend in a more conservative direction than the speeches of more liberal peers conducting the debate in the chamber.

Other arguments for the hereditary peers seem to miss the mark just as widely. Attempts to claim that they are a social cross-section of society are unlikely to succeed. A variant is that they are a purely random sample of individuals and that this in itself fits them to be legislators. The argument is negative rather than positive. As one Crossbencher put it, she hoped to hear an argument 'for it being worse than any form of selection'.[12]

The problem is that it could just as easily apply to any other group of people, and arguably would be more appropriate in a less unrepresentative group. Anthony Barnett and Peter Carty have argued for a second chamber chosen by lot, which they equate with an Athenian model from the fifth/fourth century BC.[13] There are various difficulties with this proposal, not least that almost by definition it would make into legislators a number of people who would be wholly unsuited to the task. From the point of view of hereditary peers, however, it represents a cleaner attempt at random selection than they could ever achieve as a group. There is perhaps another entertaining parallel. New Labour has been criticised by its political opponents for using representative 'focus groups' to test policy ideas; yet now it seems that some hereditary peers aspire to the same status.

Heredity is said by some peers to be a principle underlying life. The argument seems to be that it is common for some occupations to be passed on to the next generation, and that membership of the second chamber should be no different. The range of examples given has included plumbers, dockers, miners, shipbuilders and clerics.[14] With the possible exception of the latter, there is a crucial difference between training one's son or daughter in a trade and passing on to them a seat in parliament. Once they have learnt their trade, they will have the opportunity to practise it in the market place but they will succeed or otherwise by their skill; they have no right to the trade. The proper analogy is with an elected politician whose child wishes to go into politics too. The parent can teach the child some of the skills, but it is the electorate who will decide whether they wish to found a political dynasty.

The only other argument of principle which requires any kind of reply is that removing the hereditary peers from the second chamber in some way threatens the monarchy. Curiously, Lord Winston, the test-tube baby pioneer and a Labour peer, has voiced this argument.[15] Two principles are getting confused. The Government is not attacking heredity per se; it operates daily, for example, in our legal, property and family relations within society. The Government has no difficulty with hereditary peers as individuals or with the peerage as an institution. The issue is solely whether hereditary peers, or anyone else, should have a guaranteed seat in parliament which as individuals they have not earned. The role in question is that of legislator and the qualification at issue is that which best suits the role. The time when hereditary peers were naturally part of the government fabric of the country, and could claim to be integral to its constitution, is long past and so it is right to consider reform. The position of the monarch, in contrast, is central to the British constitution. Unlike the hereditary peerage, this role has not ceased to be an appropriate part of the modern constitution, which remains based on the institution of the Crown. The functions of the head of state and constitutional monarch are, moreover, quite different from those of a legislator. The Queen stands wholly outside party politics and performs a unifying function in the country unlike that of any politician. The constitutional expert, Lord St John of Fawsley has rejected any connection between the removal of hereditary peers from the second chamber and the monarchy. Nicholas Kent, a vice-chairman of the Tory Reform Group, argues convincingly that they should not be placed in the same category: while peers can exercise political power of their own free will, the Sovereign can act only at the instigation of others.[16]

Other attempted arguments of principle have included the

claim by Lord Skidelsky that the peerage is a piece of property and that its removal from the second chamber is 'the biggest act of privatisation of modern times – the biggest since the dissolution of the monasteries'.[17] His argument is that historically the peerage is a remnant of the medieval period when property carried duties at local and national levels, and that Labour should preserve it for this reason. Even he, however, does not quite argue that the hereditary peerage as an institution should continue to exercise its unique constitutional role and believes merely that some of them should remain in a reformed House. As some peers are keen to point out, the latter-day result of their former obligations is that many of them continue to give selfless public service. This is true, and they deserve praise for it, but it is not in itself an argument for them to remain in the second chamber. Public service may take many forms and will seek to be deployed by individuals wherever it is felt to be most useful.

Finally, it has even been suggested, returning momentarily to the issue of whether the House uses its powers, that hereditary peers are an advantage precisely because their presence prevents it from doing so; a fine example of a self-defeating argument.

Process

The arguments as to process are threefold and seem mainly concerned with justifying delay. The first is the familiar one from the Conservative frontbench: there should be no stage one without stage two, since once hereditary peers are removed the Government will have no incentive to go further. Those who hold this view seem to consider that this objection will largely be met if the House passes the Weatherill amendment arising from the deal agreed between the Government, Viscount Cranborne and some Crossbenchers.

The second process argument is that the stage one bill will alter the balance between the two Houses, and possibly affect the referendum on voting reform for the House of Commons, and that these wider implications need to be taken into account before it is agreed (Lord Skidelsky once again[18]). The

Government is in a position to meet these charges. It has published a White Paper alongside the bill. The Royal Commission will report in 1999. The debate is moving on to what should comprise stage two. Once this argument is voiced, it appears that the supporters of hereditary peers have fallen back to arguments of mere timing. The issue can then be fairly portrayed as to whether they should go at the beginning of the process or at the end – hardly an argument of great constitutional principle. Even they do not believe that a Royal Commission could recommend an outcome which perpetuated the hereditary peerage. On that basis, there seems to be little value in holding off the straightforward part of reform while the larger and more complex parts are settled.

Thirdly on process, Viscount Cranborne and others have sought to argue that the House of Commons should be reformed first. They claim that it fails to scrutinise legislation properly and that the job, and therefore the composition, of the second chamber ought not to be considered until the Commons have been overhauled. In a lecture, Lord Cranborne made a number of suggestions for reforming the work and structure of the House of Commons, such as reducing its size, expanding its remit to audit public expenditure and requiring governments to publish draft statutory instruments alongside the parent bill, while expressing some doubt that the Commons would be willing to undertake such reforms. He then said:

Once we have addressed the House of Commons – and only then – it would make sense to think about the House of Lords.[19]

He went on to criticise the fact that Labour had made clear its intention to proceed with Lords reform. In fact, as he later acknowledged, none of his suggestions was incompatible with the removal of hereditary peers.[20] Happily, the two aspects of Lords and Commons reform need not be quite so interdependent as Lord Cranborne suggested. Improved scrutiny or procedures in either House cannot be other than beneficial to the whole. Each chamber needs both to cover some of the same ground as the other – so that there is a 'second look' at important business such as primary legislation – while also developing distinct activities of its own. Provided that these principles are accepted on both sides, and it is understood that the procedures or even the functions of either House may need to be approached more flexibly than has been allowed to date, there need be no fundamental problem. It is important to appreciate how much the history of relations between the two Houses in the last 100 years has been coloured and distorted by the partisan nature of an unbalanced House of Lords. Failure to reform it fully at the beginning of this century left a vacuum in which ensuring the proper pre-eminence of the Commons became confused with total supremacy. The Commons has nonetheless lacked the self-confidence to distinguish between the mere expression of another view and a challenge to its authority. A more detailed understanding of the realities of governmental and parliamentary life would lead to an acceptance of a degree of give and take in the interests of consensus and good government familiar in many other countries.

Practice

The practice arguments betray a degree of self-deception about the present work of the House. It is suggested that hereditary peers bring special knowledge to the process of debate and scrutiny. In fact, on areas other than agriculture and countryside matters, it tends to be life peers who do so, particularly from the Crossbenches. It is claimed that a House without hereditary peers will be less courteous and more political. That is possible, although the House evolves constantly and it is not nearly so non-political as those who have never visited it assume it to be. Furthermore, it is suggested that the removal of hereditary peers will prevent the admission of younger members, although this could be met in various ways through a reformed composition.

More significantly, it is said that continuity will be lost, or that the work of the House will be disrupted, notably on its select committees. Obviously, if active members leave a body there may need to be a period of adjustment. On the other hand, over 500 life peers will remain, enough, it could be argued, for a parliamentary chamber to function effectively. The Cranborne/Weatherill agreement over hereditary peers addresses this argument by proposing that the House chooses a number of hereditary peers to continue in certain formal roles. The Government had anyway always made it clear that it envisaged a number of the active hereditary peers being offered the opportunity to return to the House as life peers; those hereditary members who fulfilled important roles, such as the deputy chairmen in the chamber or those who sit on their party frontbenches, would obviously have had a strong claim. In practice, the loss of continuity may be much less than some peers envisage. The Labour hereditary peer, Lord Ponsonby of Shulbrede, has produced figures which show how significant life peers have become in carrying out the day-to-day work of the House, both in the chamber and outside it. It is often thought that hereditary peers form the backbone of Lords select committees; in fact, about 70 per cent of the members are life peers.

Some hereditary peers point to the fact that the House is cheaper to run than the House of Commons because peers draw expenses but not salaries. This may be an issue to consider at stage two but it is not a reason to retain hereditary peers as such.

The practical arguments put against reform can be summed up as 'it cannot be justified but it works'. Quite apart from whether that is an acceptable basis on which to construct a chamber of parliament, the problem is that it is only partially true. The House of Lords does good and valuable work as it stands. As we have seen, however, a chamber which believes itself unable to use most of its powers cannot, by definition, be said to be working in the full sense; unless it is thought that it should not have those powers at all. If it works, it is only within constraints which to some degree extent its purpose.

We should now turn to looking at how the House actually functions. Perhaps the best way of doing this is to take a few actual instances. In some of them, the House failed to do its job properly. In others, it succeeded.

The House at work I: failing to do the job

Three examples show how its composition and political imbalance have distorted the House's role. They cover a case where the House started a job but failed to finish it, another where it failed altogether and a third where it went too far.

1. London and the metropolitan counties: the House failing to complete the job

In 1984, the House of Lords won much credibility for itself when it defeated the first stage of the Thatcher Government's abolition of the GLC and metropolitan county councils, the notorious 'paving bill' or more formally the Local Government (Interim Provisions) Bill 1984. The bill cancelled elections due in May 1985, some ten months before the planned abolition of the councils, and proposed to insert 'interim councils' of councillors from the lower-tier authorities to run the GLC and MCCs in the meantime. The Government was desperate to avoid the elections being held because they feared they would become a referendum on an increasingly unpopular policy. Yet drafting delays meant that the main abolition bill could not be introduced until the 1984/5 session and would become law well after the last date in 1984 on which the elections could be cancelled.

Nothing had been said about a paving measure in the Conservative manifesto at the 1983 general election. To make matters worse for the Government in terms of public perception, not only did a policy of cancelling elections offer enormous scope to the Government's political opponents in London and elsewhere, but the creation of interim councils in the capital and possibly Greater Manchester would pass the political control of those areas from Labour to Conservative.

It quickly emerged that, because of the deadline for cancelling the elections, the Government was intending to wait only until the Commons had passed the main bill at second reading the following autumn before activating the order to scrap the poll. To the Lords, this was seen as a constitutional outrage since at that stage they would not have approved the principle of abolition. On the latter issue, in particular, a wide coalition of Opposition and Crossbench peers pushed the Government to within 21 votes of losing a reasoned amendment at the second reading and then defeated them at the committee stage by inserting a new clause which sought to delay the cancellations of the elections until after Royal Assent had been given to the main abolition bill. The defeat was decisive (191 to 143). It took the cabinet only a week to capitulate and extend the terms of the serving GLC and MCC councillors.

It is less well known that the following year the Lords on several occasions came very close to forcing a major defeat on the main abolition legislation as well. The circumstances were different – abolition was a manifesto commitment (albeit inaccurately expressed in the document itself). For that reason, no attempt was made to defeat the central provisions of the bill. However, the two arguments stood, that unlike previous reorganisations in local government, there had been no public inquiry into the issues. Secondly, many of the functions of the old authorities would not, in fact, be devolved to lower-tier councils as the Government claimed, but would be allocated to a variety of quangos, joint boards and unelected bodies covering London and the metropolitan area. Abolition, in other words, was thought to be a political policy which would remove not only strategic local government but its public and electoral accountability.

In the Lords debates, the argument for an inquiry was quickly dismissed as a delaying measure. Attempts by Conservative rebels and Crossbenchers to create 'slimmed-down' authorities were very narrowly defeated: the London amendment moved by Lord Plummer of St Marylebone, the former Conservative Leader of the GLC, was defeated by just four votes on another large turnout (213 to 209), and the metropolitan amendment by 212 to 192.

At the time, this was assumed to be the end of the matter, but there were two stages of the Opposition parties' strategy still to come. For the rest of the committee stage, peers from all parts of the House moved amendments to maintain services at a London/county-wide level. The Government was defeated four times, on traffic and highways in London, waste disposal, conservation and the abolition of the Inner London Education Authority (which survived until 1990). By the end of committee, a combination of the Government's existing proposals and the successful amendments meant that, according to the bill as it stood, significant functions now stood to be carried out by various bodies at a London/metropolitan county level while some more local functions would be devolved to the boroughs and districts.

It was at this point that the Lords narrowly missed repeating their coup of the previous year. First, at the beginning of the report stage, the SDP peer and former local government minister, Lady Stedman, failed by just one vote to carry an amendment to retain strategic planning at the county level. Then Labour frontbench amendments from Lord Barnett sought to unite the various larger functions under one elected 'coordinating authority' in each area. Under the amendments, abolition would go ahead with the coordinating authorities inheriting only functions such as strategic planning, economic development, waste disposal and overall traffic management but running these on a democratic basis.

The Government seemed unprepared for a major turnout to meet this challenge from the Opposition, which famously came on the same day as an important social fixture, the Ascot Gold Cup. At the crucial moment, however, several factors sent the timing awry. Minor amendments on staffing remained undiscussed from the previous day's business and Conservative backbenchers, openly prompted by the Leader of the House, Viscount Whitelaw, moved them against the wishes of their sponsor and mounted a filibuster to delay the vote. The fortuitous intervention as well of a statement on a banking collapse gave the Government whips four hours to call in as many as fifty absent Conservative peers. The Opposition amendments were defeated by 17 votes (164 to 147). Staff in the House estimated at the time that if the division had taken place when planned, the amendments would have been carried by a majority of about 30 votes.

The rights and wrongs of coordinating authorities or the abolition of metropolitan county government are not the issue – although it is notable that complaints about the lack of an overall authority, at least in London, became steadily louder in the ensuing decade and the present Government is introducing legislation for a directly elected mayor and authority to undertake strategic functions. It has since come to light that the Government was indeed prepared for the possibility of a major defeat on the bill and had in mind options should a compromise prove necessary. Because of the Conservative predominance, not only was the Government able to overwhelm very substantial turnouts in favour of the earlier amendments, but at the last moment it could summon reinforcements to out-vote the bill's critics. The need for a compromise never arose on the key political controversy of the day because the second chamber, hampered by its political imbalance, never defeated the Government on the main issue. The Lords started the job of making sense of the abolition policy, but were unable to finish it.

2. The poll tax: the House failing to do the job

It is sometimes claimed that the House of Lords forfeited any claim to be regarded as a serious revising chamber when it failed to stop the poll tax in 1988. This is an over-simplistic judgement, both of the issue and of the role of a second chamber (which should surely not be able to block, as opposed to delay or modify, a manifesto commitment of an incoming government, however objectionable). On this occasion, nonetheless, there were high hopes that the second chamber would be able to follow up strong opposition from the Government benches in the Commons and adapt the bill to make it more acceptable. The ability of the Conservatives to flood the chamber with supporters put paid to this expectation, despite strong feeling among many peers.

The Local Government Finance Bill 1988 replaced domestic rates on property by a 'community charge' to raise part of local government's finance. The broad objective was that all adults should pay – where previously only householders had paid rates – in order to make local councils more accountable to their electorates, in the hope that this would exert downward pressure on their spending. The number of payers would double to 38 million, all charged the same in each local authority area except for those on income support, who would pay 20 per cent. As Michael Heseltine and many others pointed out, this meant slum dwellers and landed aristocrats, pensioners living on their savings and successful entrepreneurs all paying the same.

The bill arrived in the Lords having survived the most serious challenge to a bill in the Commons during the Thatcher era. At the Commons report stage a senior Conservative backbencher, Michael Mates MP, had moved an amendment linking the community charge to the ability to pay by banding it according to income. On 18 April 1988, after a tense debate, the amendment was defeated by a majority of 25. The scale of the rebellion rocked the Government; its majority was 100. No fewer than 38 Conservative MPs had voted against the Government and another 13 abstained. It was the worst revolt suffered by Mrs Thatcher until her deposition two years later, a fall occasioned at least in part by the political consequences of the poll tax.

It was hardly surprising that opponents looked forward to the Lords debates, particularly in the light of some celebrated defeats there on local government issues in previous years. Ability to pay dominated the second reading debate. Peer after peer criticised the list of those exempt from paying, which ignored the homeless, volunteer workers and people living in short-stay hostels. It was clear than an amendment on the lines of Mates's would be tabled and that it represented a serious threat to the Government. The Conservative Chief Whip, Lord Denham, a shrewd operator, prepared for a massive turnout.

A constitutional argument complicated the picture. Conservatives led by the former Lord Chancellor, Lord Hailsham, contended in *The Times* and elsewhere that the bill was a financial measure. Although it was not a money bill, they said, it nonetheless dealt with taxation and the powers of the House ought accordingly to be seen as limited. Opponents replied that it was a local charge, not a tax, and fell outside the money bill rules. It is probable that the raising of the argument discouraged some Conservative and Crossbench peers from voting for the amendment, despite the view of the leading constitutionalist, Sir William Wade, that the Lords 'may consider themselves entitled to "have a go" with the poll tax'[21] and an endorsement, if a careful one, at second reading from Lord Jenkins of Hillhead, historian of the 1911 controversy. In the context of reform, perhaps the larger point is that on an issue of this kind, where the House of Commons has signalled deep unease over what the government is proposing, there ought to be ways in which the second chamber can seek to respond to the concern by enabling the Commons to look at the issue again without distorting the constitutional balance between the Houses.

The long-awaited debate came on 23 May 1988 on the first amendment at the committee stage. The Conservative backbencher, the late Lord Chelwood, moved an amendment on the ability to pay. Joking that because of his name (he was the former MP Sir Tufton Beamish) he had been elected to the Tufty Club, concerned with children and road safety, he said that his amendment was a 'Stop, look and listen' amendment – not a bad one-line summary of the role of a second chamber. The amendment would have given the Government a year in which to introduce a charge taking account of ability to pay. He argued that the poll tax was widely opposed by professionals and the public and that Conservatives had always, until its advent, supported linking local liability to the ability to pay. He was supported by the former Conservative Home Secretary, Lord Carr, and former Foreign Secretary, Lord Pym. The Opposition parties, led by the Labour spokesman, Lord McIntosh of Haringey, supported his amendment. Principal opponents were the former Leader Viscount Whitelaw and Lord Hailsham. After a keen debate, the so-called 'backwoodsmen' summoned by Lord Denham gave the Government 317 votes. Lord Chelwood's combined supporters could muster only 183 (an illustration, too, of the then depleted strength in the House of the Labour and Social and Liberal Democrat parties). At the time, the vote was the second highest recorded turnout in the history of the House.[22]

The vote demonstrates two points which underline the case for reform. First, the Government would not have won and the principal objection to the poll tax – its flat-rate nature – would not have gone ahead unchallenged without the votes of hereditary peers. Second, in addition to enjoying an effective day-to-day majority, the Conservatives could now – just as in 1910/11 – call on a large number of irregular attenders, the famous backwoodsmen, to render the political imbalance even greater. It is, however, a caricature to suggest that there are hundreds of unknown peers who attend only when summoned in this way. Relatively few came to the vote who never otherwise attended, as opposed to coming occasionally. (According to the attendance record for that session, there were two who appeared only on that occasion. Such was the confusion of numbers in the chamber that three others who voted were missed and recorded as not attending and one independent peer managed to vote without having taken the oath, essential if his vote was to count.) What can be stated is that the Government's majority of 134 came from peers who were not members of the 'working House'. A total of 140 peers voting for the Government (121 Conservatives and 19 Crossbenchers/independents) were irregular attenders in that session. Most of these (99 of the Conservatives and 17 of the Crossbenchers) attended fewer than one quarter of sittings; 45 of them attended fewer than 5 per cent of sittings.

Thus was the most unpopular policy of any government in modern times voted through the second chamber. Peers still tried with partial success to alleviate some of its worst features. Amendments were inserted to give 100 per cent rebates to disabled people and higher rebates to student nurses; the former was reversed in the Commons and the latter watered down. Ministers gave a string of concessions, several of which accepted the logic of ability to pay. The homeless, remand prisoners, voluntary care workers and those suffering mental impairment since birth were exempted. After much pressure, the level of relief for charities from the accompanying business rate was also increased.

72

The poll tax lasted one year in England and Wales before its replacement was announced. A second chamber with a fairer political make-up would have required the Commons to think again about the central issue, although it is not possible to speculate further than that as to the ultimate outcome. The financial issue might well have prevented there being any prolonged confrontation between the two Houses if the Government had continued to win in the Commons. On the secondary issues, however, it seems likely that a government would have greater difficulty in getting such a bill through a House with firmer legitimacy and a fairer composition without significant amendment.

For the purposes of reform the relevant question is not a party political one: whether there should or should not have been a poll tax. The issue is one of the quality of governance. Few Conservatives would now dispute that the particular measure harmed their party and a policy which provokes riots in the capital must be of concern to all. Faced with such a challenge, the second chamber was unable because of its composition and political imbalance to perform what should have been its core role in these circumstances of giving the Commons and the Government a breathing space in which to look afresh at the proposals. It failed on this occasion even when in the Commons more than 50 Government backbenchers had defied the whips to show their concern. Instead, a policy which was widely perceived at the time to be unfair, and which proved to be all but unworkable, was ushered on to the statute book by a second chamber which had been smothered.

3. European parliamentary elections and closed lists: the House going too far

Five of the 36 Government defeats on bills in the session 1997/8 were over the European Parliamentary Elections Bill, the only piece of Government legislation not to reach the statute book in the Blair Government's first session. This recent bill serves as a case study of how 'ping-pong' and the Parliament Acts operate. It is also the exception proving the

73

rule in several respects. First, the issues at stake became much larger than those involved in most other defeats that session, which where they were led by Conservatives, were usually carefully chosen to avoid too direct a confrontation with the Commons in the run-up to Lords reform. Second, in most of the other cases, once the Commons had looked at the issue a second time, the Lords accepted the outcome (the other exception being the issue of fourth-year tuition fees at Scottish universities, where a Government compromise was accepted after the Lords had voted on the issue on three occasions). In the case of the European Parliamentary Elections Bill, the Lords voted a total of six times – reinserting their amendment four times after it was rejected by the Commons, obliging the Government to stop the bill for lack of time at the end of the session and then defeating it at second reading when it was re-presented in the following session. The issue was intrinsically political and used as a platform for the forthcoming debate on reform of the Lords.

The bill introduced proportional representation for elections to the European Parliament, which was a manifesto commitment. It was not an obvious candidate for a Lords confrontation. Unlike the bill on tuition fees (and contrary to several inaccurate reports in the press) it was first introduced in the House of Commons, so the Parliament Acts were always potentially available to the Government. Furthermore, the Conservatives, as well as the Liberal Democrats, were expected to gain European seats from the introduction of PR; perhaps as many as ten each from Labour.

Although the Conservatives opposed PR, and a number of Labour MPs were said to have misgivings, the issue was not PR but the 'closed list' system through which it would be conducted. The manifesto had not specified the system of proportional voting. Under so-called 'open' lists, the order of candidates in the region would be determined by the voters on the ballot paper, whereas under the method provided for in the bill the parties would determine the order in which their candidates would be elected. The Liberal Democrats' formal position was to favour open lists, but they supported the bill as a means to achieve PR, which was the principal fruit of their cooperation with the Government in constitutional reforms. The Home Secretary undertook to publish a study of an alternative 'Belgian' model, whereby voters choose on the ballot paper whether to vote for a party list or to rank the candidates themselves. When it appeared, the study showed that in some circumstances the addition of party votes to those cast for an individual candidate could mean that person being elected with fewer votes than another candidate.

The bill was introduced in the Commons at the end of October 1997, a full year before the crisis in the Lords with which we are concerned. Normally this would have allowed plenty of time for its passage, since a major bill generally takes about seven months to go though parliament. Three months elapsed, however, between second reading and the start of the committee stage in the Commons and the bill did not reach the Lords until spring. There, it cleared all of its stages until third reading in October by which time major debate was expected to be a formality.

Round 1: Tuesday 20 October 1998

The Opposition stayed their hand during the committee and report stages, moving amendments against closed lists but refraining from pressing them to a vote and failing to support a Liberal Democrat amendment for the Belgian system. With the session expected to end in just over a month their spokesman, Lord Mackay of Ardbrecknish, opened his attack at the third reading, normally a tidying-up stage. He moved four amendments to introduce a form of open lists which used the same system of counting by party as the Government's scheme, with parties still determining who went on to the list and their order on the ballot paper, but allowing electors to vote for individual candidates. He claimed that his system avoided the Belgian anomaly. He argued that open lists involved a democratic principle and that nine other EU states used systems which allowed electors to change the order of candidates. For the Government, Lord Williams of Mostyn pointed to the five member states, including Germany, France and Spain, which used closed lists, covering between them 70 per cent of the EU population. The last Conservative

Government had introduced a closed list system for elections to the Northern Ireland peace forum in 1996. Closed lists allowed parties to promote positively women and members of ethnic minorities as candidates. Any election under first-past-the-post presented the electorate with a closed list of one candidate from each party.

Lord Mackay pressed his amendments to a division, winning by the relatively narrow margin of 165 'Contents' to 140 'Not Contents' despite strong support from the Crossbenches and the votes of five Labour and two Liberal Democrat rebels. It was the 32nd defeat of the session, which the Government would have won by 129 to 72 on the votes of life peers alone (as they would have won all four subsequent votes on the issue, albeit by varying margins). A significant rebel was Lord Evans of Parkside, a Labour life peer and former leading member of the party's National Executive Committee, who argued strongly against its method of selecting candidates.

Round 2: Wednesday 4 November 1998
The bill returned to the Lords just over a fortnight later. The Commons' response had been emphatic. By 338 votes to 131, they had 'disagreed' with the Mackay amendments, sending back a formal Reason which stated: 'Because it would result in a voting system which is undesirable'. Lord Mackay responded with a blank counter-refusal, moving (as he would three times more) to 'insist' on his amendments. The Government Chief Whip, Lord Carter, pointed out that if the amendments were again carried, this would force the Commons to shift their ground in order to avoid losing the bill (since otherwise both Houses would have voted twice for the same separate wording). Lord Mackay argued that there was a new development in the publication of the report of the commission under Lord Jenkins of Hillhead into the voting system for the House of Commons, and he quoted from it to support his case, claiming that it justified a further division. One of the Liberal Democrat rebels, Lord Beaumont of Whitley, argued that the Lords should concede at that point. His party spokesman, Lord Goodhart, said that the bill should be supported to avoid a constitutional crisis. Lord

Evans said that the view of the Commons should now prevail and he would abstain. By 221 votes to 145, with three Labour rebels, the amendments were again carried.

Round 3: Thursday 12 November 1998
This time the Commons overturned the Lords' amendment by 307 votes to 125. The Lords considered the bill again two days later. Time was now running short, with the Queen's Speech to open the next session scheduled for 24 November and Parliament expected to rise a few days beforehand. The position, moreover, had changed. The Commons had not simply rejected the Lords' amendments but had offered an 'amendment in lieu'. So under the ping-pong procedures, each House could once again, if they wished, vote twice for the same separate forms of wording before the bill would be lost. Under the amendment in lieu, the Home Secretary would appoint a review shortly after the European election to report within six months to parliament.

This was not enough for the Opposition (even though, as Lord Evans pointed out, Lord Mackay had sought precisely such a review at an earlier stage). Notwithstanding the fact that it was unprecedented to press an amendment to a third round without offering an alternative – not least where a concession was on the table – he again moved 'insistence' on his original amendment and with it disagreement to the Commons' amendment in lieu. The amendment for the review, he said, contained no powers to change the system in response; to do so would, therefore, require a new bill. He said that Labour MPs had now voiced criticisms in the Commons. Rather than allowing parties to promote equal opportunities, closed lists could enable them to foist unpopular candidates on to the electorate. Lord Shore said that the principle was more important than that the elected House should prevail. The Liberal Democrat frontbencher, Earl Russell, said that he had changed his mind five times the previous day before deciding to continue to rebel. As a former Leader, Ivor Richard argued that the constitution relied on unwritten understandings. The second chamber might have a duty, and certainly had a right, to ask the House of Commons

77

to think again. The Commons had, however, now considered the argument again in the light of the Jenkins report and the House should now accept their view.

For Labour, Lord Williams pointed out that the Government would have won both previous votes if life peers alone had voted. The bills introducing devolution in Scotland and Wales had both included closed list systems for part of their electoral arrangements. After two rounds, the 'moral legitimacy' lay with the Commons. Lord Mackay confined his response to the issue of closed lists rather than whether it was constitutionally right to vote a third time. There was still a weekend, he said, over which the Government could produce new proposals; the Lords were scheduled if necessary to look at it again on the following Tuesday. In the division, his amendments were again supported by 237 votes to 194, a majority of 43. This time, two Labour peers and four Liberal Democrats voted with the Opposition. Counting life peers alone, the Government would have won by a majority of 57. Labour's turnout of 128, not counting the two rebels, was the second highest of the session – and highly credible given that age and ill-health mean that their nominal strength can be reduced at any time by several dozen.

Round 4: Tuesday 17 November 1998
It was now the final week before the Queen's Speech. Again, the Commons had insisted on their disagreement to the amendments, but rather than insist as well on their original amendment in lieu they proposed another. The differences were, in fact, small and show how little is required to avoid a bill becoming deadlocked during ping-pong. The new Government amendment in lieu again provided for a review – using the same wording as before – but with a new subsection added, under which the review would have been required to consider how the ability of electors to vote for a particular person on a party's list might affect the outcome of the election.

The bill was now getting into uncharted waters. The Lords had voted three times for the same proposition. The Commons had three times said no. Media interest, which was initially rather slow to pick up, was now increasing as to whether the Opposition would try a fourth time. The Opposition had already gone further than on the Scottish tuition fees issue (where, since the bill had started in the Lords, the compromise had effectively come half a round earlier). On that bill, it had been the Opposition parties in the Lords which had kept changing the wording of their amendments to avoid losing the bill. On this bill, it was the Government which was offering variants of compromise and the Opposition which kept tabling exactly the same amendments. Although the Government had the Parliament Acts' powers in reserve, it might not be possible to secure the bill's passage through the Lords in the second session in time to make the necessary administrative preparations for the new electoral system by June 1999. For these reasons, enactment in the current session would have been preferable to the Government, but the Opposition could continue to use its preponderance in the House of Lords to avoid agreement until the end of the session.

Once again, Lord Mackay moved to insist on his amendments and to disagree with the new Commons' amendment in lieu. He continued to argue on the issue of closed lists rather than the constitutional question. Defending the introduction of closed lists in Northern Ireland, he said that they had been introduced because of the special circumstances of the province and that John Major, then Prime Minister, and Tony Blair had both agreed that they were 'not ideal'. Lord Shore described the issue of the Commons against the Lords as 'bogus' since Crossbenchers had accounted for the majorities on two of the three previous Lords votes.

This time it was the former Prime Minister, Lord Callaghan of Cardiff, who appealed to the Opposition not to play games and to Crossbenchers to drop their support. The unelected House should not insist on its view four times in a row. Lord Tebbit, the former Conservative Chairman, retorted that it was up to the Government whether the bill was lost.

Lord Williams again spelt out that without hereditary peers' votes the bill would have passed and reminded the House that the Commons had approved the Government's plans five times by majorities of between 174 and 207. For the Lords to insist again on their amendments would be 'abusive of our system'. The Opposition were playing a 'stratagem'.

The Labour Party achieved its highest turnout for the session with 135 peers in the Government lobby, but although the overall vote against went up, the supporters increased by more. The House voted again for Lord Mackay by 261 to 198, again with two Labour rebels and the Crossbenchers still heavily in favour of the amendments. It was the highest turnout of the session too for the House as a whole, with 459 peers voting. Again, without hereditary peers the Government would have won by 165 to 129.

Round 5: Wednesday 18 November 1998
The timetable pressure on the Government was now overwhelming. Both Houses were due to rise on Thursday 19 November before the Queen's Speech the following Tuesday. In practical terms, one full day of business remained. On Wednesday 18, the Commons again insisted on their disagreement to the amendments, dropped their second amendment in lieu but proposed instead a third variant. The new amendment again replicated the previous wording but with the addition of a requirement on the Home Secretary to consult before appointing the person or persons to conduct the review. The same evening, the bill was returned to the Lords, who adjourned 'during pleasure' for 16 minutes to allow time to read the amendment. On their return, Lord Mackay yet again moved insistence on his amendments and disagreement to the new amendment in lieu. The issue now was whether the bill would be lost, and whether voting a fifth time would breach the constitutional conventions. Forcing that number of exchanges on a single issue was unprecedented in modern times. The possible loss of the bill, albeit through running out of time rather than as a result of being voted down, raised the Salisbury Doctrine. Lord Mackay had all along sought to argue the narrow point that, since the manifesto had been silent on closed lists, no question arose of obstructing a manifesto pledge. On a broader view, since a manifesto bill was now in jeopardy, and the policy it introduced might then be

delayed five years beyond the election it was intended to affect, the Conservatives had reached the point of breaching the letter of the convention – if they had not already passed it in spirit.

The Home Secretary, Jack Straw, in a radio interview that morning was asked about the target of the June 1999 elections. He said that if the bill was lost, reintroducing it and meeting the target under the Parliament Acts was 'not an option' without the cooperation of the Opposition. It became clear that the Government believed it needed the bill by January 1999 in order to introduce the new system in time. The cooperation of the Opposition would be needed to move the bill through its stages faster than the normal intervals allow. The reality was, therefore, that a fifth vote for the amendments would take out of the hands of the Government whether PR could be introduced by June 1999. It could secure its bill without the agreement of the Opposition in the Lords, but not sufficiently quickly to see European parliamentary elections conducted on the basis set out in its manifesto within its own term of office.

The Conservatives, and the House as a whole, clearly breached the convention in this sense. They breached it, furthermore, in spirit by continuing ping-pong on a manifesto bill for longer than anyone could remember. The then Leader, Viscount Cranborne, was known at the time to be unhappy at having been instructed by the Shadow Cabinet to vote a fifth time. Given the strain that it placed on relations between the two Houses on the eve of reform, and the dispute between Conservative peers and MPs over the Cranborne deal which erupted barely a fortnight later, to which it contributed, his reluctance can hardly be considered surprising.

Moving his amendments for the fifth time, Lord Mackay would have none of this. Removing PR from the bill would have breached the convention, he maintained, but merely insisting on open lists did not. Lord Shore said that Lord Callaghan's comments of the day before deserved an answer, which was that the Parliament Acts gave the Lords the power to vote as they proposed to do. Others, however, delivered warnings. The former Conservative minister and whip, Lord

Garel-Jones, said that the Opposition had 'tweaked the Government' but should now concede to avoid a defeat for the whole House; he questioned the motives of the Shadow Cabinet. The Convenor of the Crossbenchers, and former Speaker of the Commons and Conservative whip, Lord Weatherill, said that he had opposed closed lists on the first vote, abstained on the second and supported the Government thereafter. The second chamber should not frustrate the Commons for a fifth time; it was that fact, rather than the issue, which would be remembered. Earl Russell, who had lost his frontbench position for the Liberal Democrats over the issue, said that the House should now concede to save the bill and deliver the legislation in time. The Conservative Lord Bethell said that the Opposition would snatch defeat from the jaws of victory if they defeated the Government again. For the Government, Lord Williams made clear that the bill would fall if there were a fifth defeat; the Government would not ask the Commons to vote again, and it would be the fault of hereditary peers.

When the decision came, the vote for the amendment had fallen by nearly 50 from the day before, the Government narrowing the gap as the amendments were passed yet again, by 212 votes to 183. (Counting life peers alone, the Government would have won by 149 to 108.) The Conservatives said that they would not have won without the support of 26 Crossbenchers/independents (exactly half the number of the day before), five bishops and three Labour peers.

In fact, despite the increasing turnouts up to the fourth vote, the highest majority for the Mackay amendments was 76 on the second division. Given the size of the Conservative group, and notwithstanding the opposition of many Crossbenchers to closed lists, this perhaps betrays some of the private reluctance which many Conservative peers seem to have felt at persisting with the issue beyond the stage where the political point had been made.

The new Leader of the House, Lady Jay, announced immediately that the bill would be reintroduced under the Parliament Acts in the new session. (This was possible straight away because the twelve-month threshold from the date of the first second reading in the Commons would fall one day after the forthcoming Queen's Speech.) Royal assent would be necessary, however, by mid-January to meet the June poll. If Opposition cooperation for this was not forthcoming, the Government would proceed anyway with a view to the legislation being implemented at the poll due in June 2004. Lord Cranborne's response was widely noted:

> We are aware of the limitations on the rights of this House . . . and I hope we will behave accordingly when the bill is reintroduced.[23]

In a prologue to the major disagreement between them two weeks later, William Hague, in a radio interview the following day, effectively repudiated Cranborne's offer of a truce. So it proved. When the bill again reached the Lords in the following session, on 15 December 1998, the Opposition, in apparent breach of the Salisbury Convention, voted it down at second reading. It was then presented for the royal assent under the Parliament Acts.

In the days immediately following, there was much discussion in the press as to whether the episode had given the Government another weapon against hereditary peers or shown that the Opposition could cause trouble even for a Government with a massive majority.

From a slightly greater distance, and especially in the light of the subsequent Blair/Cranborne deal, many of the conclusions appear overheated. The Conservative Party clearly wished to scare the Government over Lords reform by underlining the scope for disruption in the second chamber. What the confrontation did show was the following:

1. The Conservatives were able to act as they did only because of the political imbalance in the House.
2. The issue (i.e., what sort of voting system was appropriate for the European Parliament) became obscured by the reality of the composition of the House, leading to a constitutional clash.
3. The episode reveals uncertainty about the proper extent of

the powers of the House and the conventions governing their use, which will need to be examined. Reform inevitably poses the question whether there should be any sort of limit on how many times the second chamber may ask the Commons to think again; or perhaps whether once a certain point has been reached a conciliation process or other defined procedure might take the issue out of the political limelight for a period and guide the actions of each House.

What all these three examples have shown is that its composition and unbalanced make-up have prevented the House from performing fully the valuable role it could have in our political discourse. It should not be thought, however, that useful revising work is not done in the present House, even encumbered as it is. The next section looks at examples of worthwhile revision undertaken by the second chamber in spite of its composition. They underline the need for, and the possible scope of, the revising role.

The House at work II: doing the job in spite of the arithmetic

Despite the impediments of its composition and political imbalance, there were examples of worthwhile concessions or changes of government policy won in the Lords among the 241 defeats suffered by the last Conservative Government. As the 1980s wore on, Mrs Thatcher's highly political approach to replacing Opposition peers meant that it became increasingly difficult for even a good argument to make an impact. Examples such as these were the exceptions – won because Conservatives rebelled, or by an ambush, or when an unusually strong argument appealed sufficiently across parties that the imbalance of forces was temporarily overcome.

Outlining some of these both gives another flavour of the work of legislative scrutiny and shows its potential. The examples quoted concentrate on defeats of government. In no sense do government upsets in the division lobbies represent more than a small proportion of the legislative work of the

House, or all of its impact (e.g., in airing issues or winning change by agreement) but they do serve to illustrate the realities of the political process of revising legislation.

As with the earlier examples, the point in each case is less whether one agrees with one side of the argument or the other than the recognition that these were legitimate questions for a second chamber to raise. The legislative and governmental process was the better for their having been raised – even if at the time the ministers concerned and their supporters took a different view. The 1980s and early 1990s were a time of very significant social and political change, much of it encouraged or even instigated by the government of the day. It is often expected of second chambers, although not always openly stated, that it is part of their role to place an occasional restraining hand on the shoulder of a government which is rushing ahead too far.

These examples include social issues, such as education and housing; democratic concerns over local government or the police; and a major question of fairness in criminal justice, the War Crimes Bill. Others could have been chosen covering the natural environment, social services, family law, civil liberties or broadcasting.

Education

In 1980, the newly elected Thatcher Government suffered a major defeat in the Lords over charging for rural school transport in the Education (No. 2) Bill. The rebellion was led by two of the most distinguished peers on the Conservatives' own benches, the senior Catholic layman, the Duke of Norfolk, and Lord Butler of Saffron Walden, who as 'Rab' Butler had introduced the Education Act which created post-war state education.

The basic issue was money. On coming into office, the Thatcher Government had sought economies in education spending, targeting school meals, milk and transport. Local education authorities bore the cost of longer journeys to school and were prohibited from charging. The proposal to remove this restriction had come from the Association of

County Councils, for whose rural members the cost of transport was highest. The policy was expected to save £20 million in that year (1980/81). There was outrage in rural areas and from the churches. Villages where the local school had been closed claimed to have been promised free transport to the nearest school. Church schools, forming about one-quarter of the system, pointed to their larger catchment areas and the disproportionate cost to parents. In vain did the minister, Lady Young, point to a series of concessions: parents on benefits would be exempt; the charges would be limited to a flat-rate; charges would cover only the first two children in a family; discretionary powers not to charge for pupils attending special schools would stay. It was no use. On 13 March 1980, after Lord Butler had said that charging would strike at 'a vital part of the concordat or settlement' which he had agreed with the denominational schools in 1944,[24] peers of all parties voted by a margin of almost two to one to delete the clause. There was no attempt to reinsert it.

A few years later, the House of Lords was instrumental in ending the use of corporal punishment in schools, following a textbook campaign by STOPP (the Society of Teachers Opposed to Physical Punishment). There were three stages. In 1985, the Government was defeated by four votes on the Education (Corporal Punishment) Bill on an amendment which would have banned it altogether. The Government dropped the bill. The following year, by just two votes, peers voted into the Education (No. 2) Bill an amendment again intended to abolish corporal punishment completely. A dispute ensued over the proper scope of the amendment and whether it should apply to the independent as well as the state sector. The Government did not concede, but rewrote the amendment in the Commons to cover all pupils in the state system and some in independent schools such as those funded under the assisted places scheme. In 1998, the Labour Government abolished such punishment in the independent sector as a whole under the Education (Schools) Act.

The imbalance in composition, and depletion of their numbers, drove the Opposition parties to use 'ambushes' to secure an occasional victory. Just before the 1992 general election, the Government was forced by the Opposition, led by Lady Blackstone, to drop controversial proposals to allow schools to choose their own inspectors. The law was also clarified as to whether, having removed inspection as a function from local education authorities, councils remained entitled to inspect their own schools.[25] Days before the prorogation for the 1997 general election, the House disabled the even more controversial provisions of the Education Bill which would have widened the use of selection at eleven. The outgoing Conservative Government dropped them in order to get other parts of the bill on to the statute book.

Public housing

In the field of public housing, the Lords made a real difference in two areas: the right to buy as it affected housing specially built or adapted for elderly or disabled people and the rights of local authority tenants facing a trust as their new landlord. The Conservatives used a series of bills from 1980 to give public sector tenants the right to buy their homes at substantial discounts.[26] The Lords inflicted ten defeats in as many years on the right to buy, six of them over this specially built or adapted housing. The concern was that this type of accommodation, on which substantial sums had usually been spent, should remain available for rent in the future rather than be sold off and have to be replaced at further high cost.

After a defeat on the Housing Bill 1980, local authorities were allowed to exclude housing for elderly people from the right to buy, subject to an application procedure to the Secretary of State. Four years later, the Government suddenly tore up these rules without consultation, inserting a new regime into its Housing and Building Control Bill at report stage in the Commons. There was an outcry from organisations concerned with housing and elderly people, to which the Lords responded by removing such housing altogether from the right to buy. Back in the Commons, the Government overturned the Lords' amendment but offered amendments in lieu allowing an exclusion for rural areas. The Lords, however, pressed their case once more and defeated the Commons' amendments by one vote. A simplified version of the status quo was agreed.

It was an uneasy compromise. The ministerial role in hearing appeals continued to prove controversial. Two years later, the Lords voted under the Housing and Planning Bill 1986 to remove it. The Government waited another three years and then fought back again under the Local Government and Housing Bill 1989. Once more ministers acted suddenly, choosing the end of the Lords committee stage to push through an amendment to remove the exclusion. Peers were angered and surprised the Government at report with an amendment of their own to restore the exclusion for existing properties, albeit with a renewed role for the Secretary of State. The Government gave in and accepted it in substance.

In the 1984 bill, the Government also proposed a right to buy for housing adapted for disabled people. It was defeated on an amendment moved by a disabled Crossbench peer, Viscount Ingleby, which was then largely accepted. Views were to change on this issue, however, among organisations representing disabled people and four years later peers voted through an amendment to the Housing Bill 1988 which removed the exclusion.

The main purpose of the 1988 bill was to start to break up local authority control of housing. Tenants would be given the right to approve in a ballot the transfer of their estate to a private landlord. The ballots were seen as biased in favour of transfer since, to prevent a new landlord taking over, a majority saying no was required, abstentions thus effectively counting as votes in favour. Attempts to make those voting arrangements more neutral were seen off by the Government whips, although an amendment to allow non-voters to stay with the authority was lost by only two votes. Tenants' representatives, however, saw as even more unfair the consultation arrangements for another type of new landlord created by the bill. Housing Action Trusts (HATs) were to bring in private money in exchange for a transfer of ownership. In a glaring disparity of treatment, the bill provided for no ballot of any kind before this type of transfer. By a margin of seven votes, Opposition peers and some Crossbenchers inserted a requirement for a prior ballot and, after some hesitation over the summer recess, the Government agreed. No HAT was, in fact, approved until 1991.

Local democracy

Two issues of local democracy where the Lords made an impact, in one case even without defeating the Government, were the accountability of the police outside London and the rights of local government officers to undertake political activities as individual citizens. While chief constables were responsible for the operational management of the police, they were accountable in England and Wales to a police authority comprising councillors and magistrates (except in London where, at present, the Commissioner answers to the Home Secretary). Under the Police and Magistrates Courts Bill 1993/4, Michael Howard inherited proposals to end the local government majority on police authorities and to place the appointment of the chairperson in the hands of the Home Secretary. Combined with powers in the bill to make easier the merger of forces, and to require chief constables to produce plans for policing in their areas, these changes were widely seen as the first step to the creation of a national police force. Academics attacked the constitutional implications and press comment was scathing. Despite strong opposition in the Lords, signalled by a debate the previous year, the Government introduced the bill there first. Crossbench peers, led by the former Home Office Permanent Secretary, Lord Allen of Abbeydale, and the former West Midlands Chief Constable, Lord Knights, joined Opposition peers, led by Lord McIntosh of Haringey and the Liberal Democrat spokesman and former Home Office Minister, Lord Harris of Greenwich, together with Conservatives including Lord Whitelaw and the former Home Secretary, Lord Carr of Hadley, to mount an overwhelming critique. Although it was soon clear that they would win a division if called, the peers deliberately stayed their hand in the lobbies. The Government caved in by stages, first making announcements and then opening negotiations with Lord McIntosh and his colleagues.

Without a single vote, the House forced the Government to remove the main objections to the bill.

In 1989, the Local Government and Housing Bill gave effect to some of the most controversial recommendations for rules governing members and committees in local government, emanating from an inquiry established in 1985 under David Widdecombe QC. His report recommended that local government officials should be banned from elected office and wider political activity. The bill contained criteria, including a salary bar of £13,500 per annum, which would have included over 100,000 middle and junior staff within the ban. Many Opposition peers agreed with the principle of a ban for higher-graded officers with policy responsibilities. This was what the report was believed to intend, but many considered that the Government had got its facts wrong and was unnecessarily narrowing civil liberties. A carefully timed vote shortly before the summer recess put the Government under some pressure of time. It became clear, again over the holiday period, that ministers would in fact welcome a compromise. Negotiations took place leading to an agreed package which raised the salary bar to £19,500 (lifting the ban from most of those threatened) and dropping the next widest category of restriction. The Lords had quietly corrected a misjudgement where ministers would have found it difficult to have given ground in the Commons.

The War Crimes Bill

The War Crimes Bill followed an inquiry into whether the law should be changed to enable alleged Nazi war criminals living in Britain to be prosecuted. Both Houses debated the issue late in 1989. The Commons voted for legislation. The Lords did not vote but the majority of speakers, including the Opposition spokesman, Lord Irvine of Lairg, opposed it.

The bill proposed that courts in this country should be given jurisdiction to try offences of murder or manslaughter (or culpable homicide in Scotland) which were committed as war crimes in Germany or German-occupied territory during the Second World War. As to the repugnance of the crimes, there was, of course, no dispute. Moving speeches were made by peers speaking on behalf of victims of the Holocaust. It was said that a vote against would be misunderstood in other countries. Other speakers recalled personal involvement in the war crimes trials which ended in 1948. The opponents of the bill questioned whether retrospective legislation was acceptable, notwithstanding that the acts were illegal under any other civilised jurisdiction and under international law; whether jurisdiction could properly be claimed; whether the punishment of a few years in jail could be considered appropriate; and whether a fair trial could be possible, given the difficulties of identification after more than forty years, and (it was contended) in circumstances where guilt was assumed. Raising the constitutional issue, Lord Irvine said that, while his personal view had not changed, he would be unhappy for the House to deny a second reading to a bill backed by an overwhelming Commons majority. After nine hours of intense debate, the reasoned amendment of the Conservative peer, Lord Campbell of Alloway, was carried by 207 votes to 74 and the bill was rejected.

When it was presented again the following April, another reasoned amendment was tabled by a Labour peer, Lord Houghton of Sowerby. (Lord Campbell tried a different route, reviving a long-disused procedure known as an Instruction to seek to extend the bill to alleged Japanese war criminals and to crimes committed by Iraqis in the Gulf War.) The bill's opponents argued that experience with similar legislation in Australia and Canada had been chaotic and failed to produce convictions. The former Lord Chancellor, Lord Hailsham, said that the fact that the Parliament Acts would ensure the bill's ultimate passage freed the second chamber to express its view. Others, however, pointed to the will of the Commons. The law lord, Lord Bridge of Harwich, found much support in arguing that it would be better to pass the bill now at second reading in the hope of amending it thereafter to strengthen safeguards against injustice. As the Government pointed out, it could still be rejected at the third reading if peers considered these insufficient. These arguments were enough to narrow the majority on Lord Houghton's amendment. The bill was, nonetheless, still rejected a second time by 131 votes to 109. It was then presented under the Parliament Acts for royal assent, becoming the first measure to be passed this way since 1949.

The War Crimes Bill was not a party political matter and was discussed under free votes in both Houses. It raised precisely the kind of important legal and moral issues on which it is right that parliament should have the widest debate and on which a second chamber, because it is not entrusted with the final decision, has a particular contribution to make. Whatever view one takes of the questions raised by the bill, it might also be agreed that, in a case of this kind, searching debate and even a delay enable the government of the day and the House of Commons to be certain that their proposed approach is the right one.

There have at the date of writing been no successful prosecutions under the act.

These examples illustrate some of the kinds of issues which a revising chamber may be asked to examine (although obviously most of the business is more concerned with matters of detail). Yet apart from War Crimes the instances here were exceptional; the composition of the House was overcome. In many other cases it was not, underlining the need for reform.

None of these examples should be taken to imply that MPs in the House of Commons were laggardly or did not appreciate the issues concerned. In most cases, the bills concerned had started there and – at least on the more political issues – similar amendments had been moved but defeated by the government majority. The point is that in a more fluid situation, where the stakes are less high, there is sometimes scope among the dozens of issues which are raised on any controversial bill for something which deserves a greater hearing to surface.

That scope will remain, or even be enhanced, by reform. The gain will be in the quality of law-making. Labour proposes a House in which the government of the day will not have a majority. Outside groups will still be able to bring a good case before the second chamber with a greater hope of success than is sometimes possible in the Commons. This need not be a serious setback for a government confident of its bill. Indeed, the process of scrutiny in the second chamber ought ultimately to strengthen the hand of government by securing stronger consent for its measures.

Furthermore, after reform, even where the second chamber did press a point, the Commons should, of course, retain the ultimate right to decide the issue. Depending on the model and its political arithmetic, the second chamber would probably be unable to push an issue strongly unless there were a degree of consensus across parties or groups. It is only where a reformed second chamber was in the right that it could be seriously troublesome to a government. Otherwise, where there is no strong outside feeling, the process of overturning amendments takes very little time, often a matter of only minutes in each House. A serious chamber would also doubtless wish to ration itself to maximise its impact. It would be wrong, for example, to draw too many conclusions about the future from the trouble which the present House has caused over the European Parliamentary Elections Bill. The point of these examples from recent history is to underline that there is a proper role for a second chamber which can take a more independent view. In our view, this is unlikely to happen unless, and until, the issues of legitimacy and credibility are resolved.

PART TWO

MOVING TO REFORM

CHAPTER THREE

THE GOVERNMENT'S APPROACH

THE STARTING GUN for Lords reform was fired on 20 January 1999 when the Government announced its package of proposals for stage one and beyond. The bill to remove hereditary peers was published. At the same time, the Government announced the chairman and terms of reference of a Royal Commission which would sit while the stage one bill was being debated and report by the end of 1999. The case for reform and the issues for the Royal Commission were set out in a White Paper entitled 'Modernising Parliament: Reforming the House of Lords'.[1]

The House of Lords Bill

The House of Lords Bill contains just five clauses and a short schedule (a legislative appendix). It provides that after enactment no one be a member of the House of Lords by virtue of a hereditary peerage (clause 1). As a result, the bar on those peers voting for, or being elected to, the House of Commons will be removed (clause 2). Clause 3 and the schedule deal with the consequential repeal of parts of the Peerage Act 1963, allowing the right to renounce a hereditary peerage to remain but under a different procedure. The bill will come into effect, and the writs of summons of hereditary peers cease to have effect, at the end of the session in which the bill is passed (clause 4). The Government hopes that this will be by autumn 1999. (To enable hereditary peers to go on to the electoral register in time for elections next year, however, part of clause 4 will come into effect immediately on royal assent.) Clause 5 clarifies that the bill extends to the Prince of Wales.

The explanatory notes to the bill make clear that the royal dukes as well as the Prince of Wales will cease to sit in the Lords. Other hereditary peers of first creation will also be excluded (but they were offered life peerages on the day the bill appeared). Viscount Cranborne, who under a process known as 'acceleration', holds a seat before inheriting his full title, will also be excluded. Hereditary peers will lose the privileges of membership of parliament. They will lose the right to allowances and the use of the facilities of the House, such as its library and restaurants (although the notes make a point of saying that the House could grant this right to a hereditary peer) and their exemption from jury service. Their titles, and any other rights connected with membership of the House, would be unaffected. There would be no impact on archbishops and bishops, serving and retired law lords or life peers. There would be no effect either on the position of the Queen, who is not a hereditary peer.

Slightly surprisingly, the Government said that it did not expect any significant savings from the Bill, in terms of peers' expenses and daily allowances, the argument apparently being that many of those who will be removed attend only rarely.

The Royal Commission

The Royal Commission was established quickly and asked to report by 31 December 1999 (giving the lie to the assumption that such bodies take years to complete their work). In a move which caused general surprise, the chairman was announced as the Conservative peer Lord Wakeham, Chairman of the Press Complaints Commission and a former Leader of both Houses and Chief Whip in the Commons. Not known for a long-standing interest in constitutional reform, his reputation was rather that of 'Mr Fixit', a political operator par excellence. Another member is to be the former Labour minister and Chairman of the Select Committee on Culture, Media and Sport, Gerald Kaufman MP. Other members were announced later.

The terms of reference of the Royal Commission were as follows:

> Having regard to the need to maintain the position of the House of Commons as the pre-eminent chamber of parliament and taking particular account of the present nature of the constitutional settlement, including the newly devolved institutions, the impact of the Human Rights Act and developing relations with the European Union:
> – to consider and made recommendations on the role and functions of a second chamber;
> – to make recommendations on the method or combination of methods of composition required to constitute a second chamber fit for that role and those functions;
> – to report by 31 December 1999.

The primary point was expressed to be the maintenance of the position of the Commons, which immediately gave the task of the Royal Commission a practical political edge. The linkages to devolution, the Human Rights Act and the EU all contained pointers to certain types of outcome, although it should not be assumed – as we shall see – that there is only one model which would meet these tests.

The connection between composition, role and functions was made explicit, at least so far as the terms of reference were concerned (but see below on White Paper, Chapter 8). The powers of the Lords, however, were not expressly referred to, although Lord Wakeham immediately made it clear that he considered the terms of reference wide enough to encompass consideration of the issues 'in the round'.[2]

The Government wishes the Royal Commission to consider all options for reform consistent with its terms of reference.[3] Contrary to expectations, however, the Government itself will not give evidence to the Royal Commission, although the Labour Party and presumably other political parties will do so.

*

Given the complexity of these issues, we should try to be as clear as possible as to what the White Paper says and – perhaps as importantly – what it does not say.

The White Paper

The White Paper takes the form of eight chapters with a foreword by the Prime Minister. The early chapters set out the history and the present position, the Government's approach and the proposals for the Royal Commission and the transitional House. In Chapters 7 and 8, however, the document summarises some of the factors surrounding stage two which the Royal Commission is to address.

Although the executive summary contains no statement of a government preference, and the document states that no 'advance prescription' is to be given to the Royal Commission,[4] these final two chapters were widely seen as containing, in the way they are written, a not too subtle steer towards a combination of nomination and indirect election. In an interview with the *Financial Times* two days after the White Paper was published, Lady Jay gave what was described as a 'strong hint' that this was what the Government wanted.[5]

Moving to stage two

The White Paper aims to tackle at the outset the criticism that there will never be a second stage. In his foreword, Tony Blair sets out the Government's pledge:

> New Labour in government will, as we promised, carry out a careful and considered reform of the House of Lords: the immediate removal of the hereditary peerage, and longer-term reform of the House of Lords as a whole.

This is repeated later in the document. The Government wants to see a 'modern, fit and effective' second chamber and, although the removal of the majority of hereditary peers will be a radical step, 'it will be followed by further reform'.[6]

Timing of stage two

The timing, set by the Government, is very tight and cannot be regarded as certain. The executive summary states that the Royal Commission is being asked to report quickly to enable the Government to make every effort to ensure that stage two has been 'approved by parliament by the time of the next general election'. The press were briefed to this effect on the day of the announcement.[7] The same thing is said in Chapter 5 of the White Paper, subject to the caveat that the Government would make every effort 'if there is consensus'.[8] A different formulation appears, however, in the following chapter which says merely that the deadline will 'allow the Commission's recommendations to be considered by the Government and the other political parties in advance of the next general election', i.e., appear in their manifestos. Two days after the announcement, Lady Jay was reported as indicating that legislation by the next election was unlikely, although not to be ruled out.[9]

Relationship with the House of Commons

The White Paper sets out the Government's view that two chambers are necessary but that the second chamber should not usurp the first. In an important section,[10] it spells out the distinctions which underpin the superiority of the House of Commons. As we have seen, these are that the Lords has no influence over the choice of who forms the government, has no powers over taxation and spending and operates within the constraints of the Parliament Acts. It suggests a fourth, that members of the Lords have no constituency representative functions. It is undoubtedly the case that the role of MPs in representing single member constituencies, giving the electorate direct access to government through an individual representative, is a key feature of the primary chamber. We shall return to that issue later.

Writing these factors into the work of the Royal Commission in this way is extremely helpful. It focuses the debate, and ought to give the Commission the confidence that it can examine all the options on the basis of a starting point shared by all those involved. Its recommendations, furthermore, will be founded on those explicit principles, adding to their weight in terms of future constitutional practice.

Stage one process

The White Paper sets out in detail the Government's step-by-step approach. The right of hereditary peers to sit and vote will be removed by the bill. A transitional House will result, containing mainly life peers. The Royal Commission will then make recommendations for longer-term reform. As stated in the manifesto, a joint committee of both Houses would then be asked to examine the parliamentary aspects in more detail. It too will be asked to work quickly.

The Cranborne/Weatherill agreement

The Government states in the White Paper that it is 'minded to accept' at an appropriate point in the bill a Crossbench amendment to provide for one in 10 hereditary peers (i.e., 75) plus some office holders to stay until the next stage. This proposal was developed on the Crossbenches by the Convenor, Lord Weatherill, with the Earl of Carnarvon and Lord Marsh. It was Lord Cranborne's willingness to agree to it with the Prime Minister on behalf of Conservative peers which led to his peremptory dismissal by William Hague.

As the White Paper puts it, the advocates of the amendment believe that it would enable the bill to be 'agreed consensually' and 'without any threat of deliberate frustration' of the rest of the Government's programme by hereditary peers.[11] Lord Weatherill has said that he sees it as providing continuity in the work of the House. Announcing the White Paper, however, Lady Jay and Margaret Beckett, the Leader of the Commons, made it clear that the Government's view of the amendment depended on whether the 'normal conventions' would be observed; a 'pitched battle' would jeopardise the deal. With Lord Cranborne's dismissal, of course, there is now no formal deal with the Opposition frontbench in the

Lords. The Conservatives have said, however, that they will support the amendment but that in effect this need not prevent them from seeking to amend the bill in other ways.

If the amendment was agreed, hereditary peers would be chosen by electoral colleges of the differing parties and groups, shared out according to their proportionate strengths among those peers. The Conservatives would choose 42, Labour 2, the Liberal Democrat 3 and the Crossbenchers 28. Added to this total of 75 peers, a further 14 would be elected by the House as a whole, probably drawn from those hereditary peers who serve currently as deputy speakers, chairmen and deputy chairmen. Finally two hereditary holders of royal offices, the Earl Marshal and the Lord Great Chamberlain, would also remain until stage two, producing a total of 91 hereditary peers.

Party balance in the transitional House

The Government says that in the transitional House it will ensure that no one party will have a majority. To do this, the Government's present plan is to seek only 'broad parity' with the Conservatives. The White Paper points to the manifesto objective of ensuring that 'over time party appointees as life peers more accurately reflect the proportion of votes cast at the previous general election'. It says, however, that there will be 'for the time being no changes to the conditions attached to life peerages' (an oblique reference to the absence from the White Paper of any proposals for a retirement age or an attendance requirement) and that, in consequence, progress towards the manifesto formula must largely be carried out by creating new peers.[12] In the transitional House, however, the principles of broad parity between the two largest parties and proportionate creations from the Liberal Democrat and other parties would be maintained. The Crossbenches would be maintained at about their present proportion (c. 25 per cent of life peers).

This approach may, however, benefit from further refinement. As a consequence of the Weatherill amendment, if it is agreed, the number of Labour peers needed to achieve parity will be increased by over 40 (i.e., from what it would have been if the Government were seeking to match only the Conservatives' total of life peers). There may be two arguments which the Government needs to answer arising from this: that the large number of life peers to be created could complicate a transition to a different model for stage two; and that Labour would eventually hold a voting majority among life peers once the 91 hereditary peers had departed. This could be answered, for example, if the majority of the incomers were willing to undertake to stand down (if a means were introduced) or otherwise to take continuing leave of absence at stage two. This would effectively put them into the same position as the 91 hereditaries and automatically maintain parity among life peers as the House moved into stage two. It would also remove the danger that the Royal Commission might feel constrained as to its recommendations. It may be, however, that the 42 continuing Conservative hereditary peers will themselves be offered life peerages. If so, then this arithmetic remains.

Some creations would clearly be necessary. It will be important that Labour's 17 peers with inherited titles[13] are offered the opportunity to continue their service in the transitional House. With two places available under the Weatherill amendment, however, this need imply no more than 15 creations.

The Government's desire to seek parity is wholly understandable. For it not to match the Conservatives' total, even for a temporary period, would require clear understandings from the Opposition as to their behaviour in the transitional House. On the other hand, from the Government's point of view, forgoing such an advantage would be another earnest of its intention to move to stage two. Were the Opposition to refuse to offer sufficient guarantees of their own good behaviour to make it possible, they could be seen as obstructing progress towards the second stage.

The most constructive development would be if all parties and groupings undertook not to seek any significant increase in their total numbers of life peers until the future composition of the House was decided. A voluntary arrangement which effectively limited most creations to the period of the transitional House would be desirable and could also be taken up by other parties.

Whatever the outcome, the issue points to the tension inherent in making what could be permanent arrangements – the creation of a significant number of life peers – in a transitional House whose replacement, according to the White Paper, may have been enacted within two to three years.

Appointments Commission

An independent Appointments Commission will take over from the Prime Minister the role of recommending non-political appointments. It will also assume the task of vetting party nominees as to propriety (e.g., as to political donations), a function currently performed by the Political Honours Scrutiny Committee. In effect, it seems that the Prime Minister will continue to control the numbers but no longer the names. While he will determine, as now, the number of nominations to be made to the Queen, he will ask the Commission for the same number of names and pass them on to her. In the same way, he has undertaken to pass on the recommendations of other party leaders to fill their vacancies. Only in highly exceptional circumstances (the White Paper mentions a danger to the security of the realm) will the Prime Minister directly influence any nominations outside his own party. Once the Commission has passed a nomination the Prime Minister will have no right to refuse it.

The Commission will be made up of representatives from the three main parties with a majority of independent members, including the chairman. Members will themselves be appointed in accordance with the rules of the Commissioner for Public Appointments. It will be an advisory non-departmental body. The public will be invited to make nominations for the much-publicised 'people's peers' (although the phrase does not appear in the White Paper). The qualities and information sought will be published. The Commission will encourage suitable bodies to make them and will be expected to encompass a broader field than at present. The potential of this body may prove to be great: it is, after all, the first time that a prime minister has voluntarily limited his power of patronage in relation to the Lords. As such, it should be reassuring.

Role and functions

The White Paper lists the functions of the Lords (revising legislation, questioning ministers, debating matters of interest and investigating through select committees), but significantly makes no reference to any constitutional role of providing a check and balance to the power of the executive or acting as a 'constitutional longstop' as it was seen to do in the 1980s (other than its veto over a bill to extend the life of a parliament). This omission is repeated later when the functions and powers are examined in greater detail.[14] It is perhaps surprising, in the light of the Bryce Commission's view, that the delaying power of the second chamber was especially important for constitutional bills. The role of looking at issues not of interest to the Commons is also omitted.

The White Paper argues in Chapter 4 that the House of Lords has no functions separate from those of the Commons other than its judicial work. This is not, of course, unusual among second chambers. A large part of their role is to review legislation and government business. The Lords perform activities such as debating issues which are sensitive or not of interest to the Commons, or undertaking in-depth examination of European issues. Their scrutiny of proposed ministerial powers in bills, before they are debated, is not a task shared with the Commons.

Second chambers overseas

The White Paper says that the pattern of second chambers overseas ranges from wholly nominated to wholly elected. It looks at five examples; we should as well.

Canada

The Canadian Senate is wholly nominated (it is, in fact, the

106

only example in the Western world). Its 104 members are appointed by the Governor-General on the advice of the Prime Minister and serve until retirement at 75. Originally intended to fasten together the federal system, it gives equal representation to French- and English-speaking provinces. It is claimed to have a high reputation for its select committee reports and to investigate bills before they are sent from the Commons. As the White Paper says, however, there have been proposals for its reform for sixty years.

The reasons for this can be found in the report on it from the independent Constitution Unit.[15] This found that although members nominally represent provinces, appointments are actually made on a party political basis. It has strong powers but rarely uses them because to challenge an elected house would be seen as undemocratic. There is cynicism among Canadians because of the appointments system. It enjoys little respect and its work is ignored or even ridiculed in the media. It presents a clear example of the link between composition and powers.

In the same report, the Unit draws attention to the experience of New Zealand. The constitution of 1854 was modelled on the British system, with a lower house elected by first-past-the-post and an appointed upper house. There was much criticism of patronage and party political appointments, especially after a move to renewable terms of office. In 1914, legislation was passed to move to proportional elections for the second chamber but it was postponed because of the First World War and never introduced. Instead, abolition became a political issue and was enacted in 1950, allegedly as a temporary measure. New Zealand is still unicameral.[16]

Germany

The German upper house (Bundesrat) has 69 delegates from the federal states (Länder). Smaller states are over-represented. Votes are cast for each state as a block and officials act as alternates because of the commitments of their political chiefs. Länder implement approaching 60 per cent of federal legislation.

It is doubtful whether Germany holds many lessons for the

second chamber in the UK. As the White Paper says, the primary purpose is to represent Land governments, as opposed to their assemblies. The nearest equivalent in scale to a Land government would be Scotland after devolution, but English regions will in no sense be equivalents. We shall look in the next chapter at the implications for devolution and accountability of having members of such bodies in the reformed second chamber, but it is worth noting two points at this stage. First, it would be inconceivable in the UK parliamentary system for single-party delegations, as are sent to the Bundesrat, to be considered as representative. (Sending a politically mixed delegation, on the other hand, would weaken the standing of the executive group at home.) Second, representation of the devolved institutions would reopen the question of whether devolved areas of policy should be scrutinised in a second chamber and might be seen as taking powers back to Westminster (as in fact it would be).

As the White Paper points out, the principal contribution of the Länder is through officials in the committee stage. The process is essentially one of consultation and negotiation between governments at federal and state level, rather than a representative political process. It must be doubtful whether the UK government would wish to mediate its detailed discussions with the devolved executives through a second chamber, especially one which is likely to be much larger than a committee of the Bundesrat and with a composition which also includes independent and political members.

Ireland
The Irish Senate is largely indirectly elected, with a small appointed element. There are 49 indirectly elected members, drawn from six functional constituencies: culture and education (including law and medicine), agriculture, labour, industry and commerce, public administration and social services, and the two ancient universities. The electorate for the last constituency are graduates of the universities, but otherwise the electors are the members of the lower house, and county and borough councillors, and the outgoing Senate. The result, as the White Paper says, is that in practice the elections are

highly politicised. The 11 nominated seats are meant for people of high calibre who would not stand for election but seem to be usually taken by politicians.

The Senate has very limited powers and it rarely suggests changes to legislation.

France

The French Senate is indirectly elected by about 145,000 local *notables* who are often local councillors. Its 321 members serve for nine-year terms with elections every three years and are seen as representing territorial areas. Rural areas are over-represented. The White Paper points out that most members see their role as lobbying the government (i.e., on behalf of their areas) rather than acting as legislators. (This system of using representative positions as bases for informal lobbying is characteristic of the French governmental system at all levels. Whether it would be welcome in Whitehall is perhaps a moot point.)

The Senate has quite wide theoretical powers which could produce deadlock with the lower house, the National Assembly. In reality, however, it is the executive which has the strength over the parliament as a whole. It can bypass the Senate by referring a dispute to a joint committee of both Houses. If it agrees with the result, it becomes law. If it does not, or no agreement is reached, the most recent version passed by the lower house is enacted without the Senate's agreement.

USA

The United States Senate is directly elected with two senators from each state (although it was originally indirectly elected by the state assemblies). The White Paper points out that it is the only second chamber which is as powerful as the lower house (thereby underlining that all other wholly elected second chambers are weaker than their primary counterpart).

As the White Paper says, its purpose is to represent the states in the Union. It is worth noting that it does this as a directly elected rather than an indirectly elected body.

The Senate has all the powers of the House of

Representatives except that it cannot initiate money bills (although it may refuse them). In addition, it alone approves key federal appointments and ratifies foreign treaties. What this demonstrates is that its standing *vis-à-vis* the House is a matter of powers; which in turn is a matter of choice as to how the constitutional structure is designed. In a presidential system, moreover, the lower house lacks the authority that it has in a parliamentary one where the government derives its authority from that chamber. So while the distinctions between the UK and US systems clearly prevent any direct parallels, the differences serve to underline that there is nothing intrinsic in the relationship between two Houses of a legislature where both are directly elected which prevents one from being superior to the other. Where their legitimacy is equal, the balance between them is a matter of the choices made as to their respective powers.

It is interesting that of the five examples chosen in the White Paper, three are indirectly elected when fewer than a third of second chambers overall have that basis.[17] What is striking, however, about the indirectly elected examples, as well as the appointed one, is their weakness as revising chambers. The Irish Senate rarely makes suggestions; the French is focused elsewhere; the Canadian lacks the legitimacy. The White Paper suggests no evidence of fitness for the principal purpose – at least of a type relevant to the UK system – which can be drawn from these examples of indirect election or nomination.

The exception, at least in terms of its strength, is the German Bundesrat, but it is not a representative body in the Westminster sense. It derives its status from being the delegate body in which powerful state governments are represented at national level in a federal system. In that context, their position is enhanced further by being the delivery mechanism for much of the federal government's legislation. Its main power is over legislation affecting the regions, which it may block. It plays little role in the political affairs of the country as a whole, and where it has no blocking powers it may only make recommendations. The German federal system and its structures are very far from being a paradigm for the unitary UK, even in the brave new world of devolution. The equivalent here would be to scrap the second chamber in favour of a bureaucratic body of a few dozen members in which the ruling group in each of the devolved institutions and regional assemblies sat to review the impact of government legislation on their areas, with their chief executives wielding the voting card. Aside from the problem of the differing responsibilities of the various bodies, it hardly seems likely that the Government would wish to move in such a federalist direction. Its applicability to the issue of the UK's second chamber must, therefore, be regarded as limited.

Examples of other countries whose second chambers are wholly or largely directly elected include Australia, Belgium, Brazil, the Czech Republic, Italy, Japan, Mexico, Spain and Switzerland.

The Government's view of the issues

In the final two chapters of the White Paper, the Government sets out some of the issues it considers lie behind the role, powers and composition of a second chamber. Although it opts explicitly for no specific model, it sets parameters and includes pointers.

Role of the second chamber

Legislative scrutiny
The second chamber, says the White Paper, should 'continue to complement' rather than duplicate the House of Commons.[18] Without the Lords' legislative scrutiny, the burden on the Commons would be greater and the quality of government legislation diminished. It would continue to be an important purpose of the second chamber.

As the government document the White Paper cannot, of course, be expected to criticise the policy of a previous administration, at least not too overtly. Institutionally, governments rarely admit they are wrong. In our previous chapter, however, were a number of examples where the second chamber did, or did not, improve what many regarded at the time as bad legislation. To read the White Paper, one might assume that a government had never been challenged, and occasionally even defeated, in the second chamber; that it and the rest of parliament existed principally to support what the government of the day was doing. Perhaps not surprisingly, nowhere is it expressed or acknowledged that a second chamber is, and should be, a check and balance on the executive, that a powerful executive needs to be balanced and that revision must on occasion be capable of becoming resistance, for otherwise it has no credibility. Resistance should only go so far, and a government with the Commons behind it must ultimately be capable of getting its way. No worthwhile reform will emerge, however, if these basic realities are shirked. It is the responsibility of the Royal Commission to address them and of ministers to acknowledge them.

Representing the regions (or regional bodies)
The White Paper points out that by the time the second chamber can be fully reformed, there will be devolved institutions in Scotland, Wales and Northern Ireland. London will have a directly elected authority. Regional Development Agencies will have been introduced and regional chambers created and some regions may be working towards regional assemblies of their own.

Regional chambers will be non-statutory groupings including local councillors and business representatives. The Government's policy is to introduce regional assemblies in the future only where there is a demand in a particular region, expressed in a referendum.

The relationship of the second chamber to these bodies should, it says, be a 'significant part' of the Royal Commission's deliberations, which could affect both the functions and membership of the second chamber. Any relationship with the second chamber would presumably need to sit alongside a link between the House of Commons and English regions. The Leader of the Commons, Margaret Beckett, has already announced, for example, the re-creation of a select committee in which English MPs may pursue regional issues.

The key question asked is whether the second chamber should have 'some overt role as the representative of the regions, or of the regional bodies', referring to the example of the French Senate.[19] The question may unlock the identity of the reformed second chamber and what it represents. In the choice it poses, however, between representing 'regions' and 'regional bodies' lies a crucial distinction which we shall explore in the next chapter. It is the choice between representing people and representing institutions.

The White Paper also raises the question of whether MEPs, who from June 1999 will be elected on a regional basis, should have a role of some kind in relation to the second chamber. It is mooted that this could reinforce its regional links and improve connections between Westminster and Strasbourg. The suggestion does not appear to be that MEPs as a whole should serve in the second chamber (an old idea in circulation from the days before they were directly elected). With the development of the role of an MEP in recent years, and with it their commitments in Brussels, Strasbourg and their constituencies, this would not be a realistic option in terms of the time they would have available and would detract from their primary role.

Rather, the suggestion seems to be that they should choose a limited number of nominees. Apart from time, any proposal for membership would need to recognise that while there are some similarities between the roles, there are also key differences. The jobs are not the same. The separation of the Commission from the Parliament, and the dominant role of the member states in the Council, means that MEPs have a more insulated role from the source of executive power than would members of the second chamber. European legislation, moreover, is written according to the principles of codified law, requiring a wholly different approach to its scrutiny geared more to the broad thrust of policy than to the detailed consideration of the drafting.

Like other such proposals for the membership of a second chamber, giving seats to MEPs would need to be weighed against the drawbacks that it confuses public accountability and asks people to perform two jobs. Improving links, on the other hand, could offer significant benefits in drawing the processes of scrutiny together. It could include mechanisms for liaison between named members in each body. Shared experience and joint working could improve scrutiny of two very different executive bodies, in Brussels and Westminster, and bring European issues to domestic attention at a formative stage.

Functions of the second chamber

The White Paper says that the Royal Commission should look at the functions of the present House of Lords and whether they are necessary. Once again, it describes these as legislative, deliberative, interrogative and judicial with no reference to any constitutional aspect in the scrutiny of legislation or, in an inherent sense, as a check and balance on the executive.

Legislative
The White Paper states:

> the Government believes that a reformed House of Lords must have the legitimacy to ensure the value of its recommendations for improvements to legislation.[20]

This is clearly right. If it did not have legitimacy, nor could offer a 'distinctive and informed view', it would not be successful. This is an important statement of the standing which should be sought for the second chamber in order to fulfil its core role.

The document also draws attention to a difficult issue. As it says, there is a potential tension between the traditional role of revising legislation and the possible new one of acting as 'the hub of a representative institutional network'. As it points out, such roles co-exist in some other countries, but in those cases the regional institutions will generally stand in the same relationship to the centre. In the UK, when the devolved institutions take over their functions, Westminster will have different powers in relation to different parts of the country. English regions will not be law-making bodies and their responsibilities will in no degree parallel the domestic range of the Scottish Parliament over, for example, such areas as health, higher education, most civil and criminal law, or agriculture.

There are major difficulties in securing similar representation from such bodies where devolution is asymmetrical. There is also the possible impetus in a federal direction which such representation might cause. The White Paper itself, however, points to a possible resolution. It says that Spain provides perhaps the nearest example of developing regional identity through devolution rather than federalism, and at different speeds in different regions. More than four-fifths of the Spanish Senate is, however, directly elected at present with less than one-fifth indirectly elected by the regional assemblies. Direct election – because it routes accountability to voters through the ballot box rather than to institutions with differing powers and functions – can avoid most of the complications and provides those elected with a common basis of legitimacy.

Deliberative

The White Paper says that the Lords has always seen as important its ability to provide advice and initiate debates on important issues. The likely presence of expertise, it says, gives these debates 'an authority they might not otherwise have'. The Government wants this function to continue in a 'distinctive' fashion. This obviously underlines the value of the Crossbenchers; it perhaps says rather less for the contribution of political life peers.

The document praises the select committee work of the House, which it recognises as distinct from that of the Commons, and hopes that it will continue and expand. It sees value in the work of the Delegated Powers and Deregulation Committee in examining the extent of ministerial powers in bills. It also says that scrutiny of EU legislation is important and could be expanded and that there is scope for wider analysis of the effect of EU policies. It again mentions a role for MEPs. In this area, formalised joint working could be most beneficial.

Interrogative

The White Paper takes the view that ministers should continue to sit in the Lords, both to allow the revising role to be more effective and to allow the second chamber to question the 'Crown in Parliament' directly.

Judicial

The document says that it is unusual in a major democracy for judges to sit in the legislature and says that it would be legitimate for the Royal Commission to consider this issue, although its terms of reference would not allow it to make detailed proposals for an alternative final court of appeal. Factors would include the effect of their removal on the nature of parliament and the need to relocate the senior judiciary elsewhere in the system. It explains that the law lords' place as life peers, rather than ex-officio members, is rationalised in the present day by their contribution on retirement to the scrutiny of legislation and to debate on legal matters.

Religious representation

No change is proposed in the transitional phase in the position of Church of England bishops. The number of bishops, says the White Paper, is justified because of their duties elsewhere. The Government will look for ways to increase the representation of other religious traditions and in particular of the Church of Scotland, which is established but has never had representation as of right. (These suggestions also imply the creation of more life peers in the transitional house.) In a longer-term reform, legal and practical obstacles to granting other faiths regular representation as for the bishops should be examined. When the statement was announced, the Bishop of Chichester confirmed that this was acceptable to the Church of England.[21]

Powers

The White Paper explains the way in which the Lords' lack of

116

legitimacy has led them to constrain the exercise of their formal powers by means of convention, including the Salisbury Convention. It says that this has generally produced a workable relationship with the Commons, and suggests that by 'institutionalising the understandings' the formal powers could remain intact but be subject to codified conventions as to their exercise.

It prefers, however, to reduce the powers, sensibly accepting that this might lead to their being used more frequently. While it recognises this connection, it omits any reference to the link between composition and powers. It lists the areas which would need to be considered, but makes no firm proposals for:

- the length of the delaying power
- removing the veto from bills first introduced in the Lords
- changing the procedures where the Lords insist on amendments rejected by the Commons (i.e., whether it could vote a second or subsequent time)
- introducing a conciliation process between the two Houses
- substituting delay for the veto on statutory instruments

It also suggests that while the House should determine its own procedures, the Royal Commission might like to make recommendations. It no doubt has this in mind when it earlier explains that, unlike the Commons, the Lords is a self-regulating body in which government business has no priority and where decisions on the conduct of business and debate are taken by agreement.

Composition of a reformed second chamber

In the final chapter of the White Paper, the mood changes. A highly readable document becomes tense and opaque. This is regrettable, since in many ways this is the most important part of the document.

The principal task of the Royal Commission, it says, is to recommend a future composition. It discusses different models for composition, although, rather as with powers (and

117

despite the White Paper's own claimed approach), the inter-connectedness of membership with role and functions is not really drawn out. It suggests that a combination of types might be the best way of creating a body fitted to its function, pointing out that several overseas chambers have a 'part-nominated, part-elected structure'.[22] Repeatedly, and confusingly, in this chapter, the White Paper uses 'elected' to cover indirectly and directly elected bodies.

In what could be regarded as a hint to the Royal Commission to look for minimal change, it says that the Commission will wish to take account of the 'more attractive features' of the present House, in which it includes the Crossbench element, the expertise of individuals and those who have given 'distinguished public service as politicians' (i.e., party life peers).[23]

Clearly thinking of schemes such as the Athenian lottery, it says that many reform schemes have been brought forward, but that in the Government's view 'the best solution is likely to be found among the more conventional options of nomination and election'.[24]

It sets out four principal models:

- a nominated chamber
- a directly elected chamber
- an indirectly elected chamber
- a mixed chamber

As we shall see, there are several types within the fourth model and the distinction between direct and indirect election frequently becomes blurred. These four options deserve more detailed discussion. It could well be that they encapsulate the issues which in the end will prove most controversial in the whole process of reform.

Nominated chamber

Although, as the White Paper acknowledges, the much criticised Canadian Senate would be the only other example, it describes a nominated House as a 'possible future model'. The distinction between the present and transitional Houses is that the process of appointment will no longer be totally controlled by the government (although it will apparently continue to control the overall numbers). It believes, nonetheless, that this distinction is sufficient to serve as a possible 'basis for an alternative model for a nominated House'.[25] This leads it immediately to discuss how the appointments mechanism could work, rather than to examine any of the broader issues surrounding the suitability of a nominated House.

For independents, it says that the first option would be to continue with a central appointments process, encouraging both self- and public nominations and asking the appointments body to search positively with interest groups and professions, though on the basis of making suggestions rather than nominating directly. As an alternative it canvasses 'functional constituencies' under which individual professions would have the right to nominate direct. It acknowledges, however, the danger that their representatives would become delegates or intervene only where 'mandated' to do so, and that such constituencies have become politicised in Ireland and were controversial in Hong Kong.

For political members, the White Paper betrays concerns that nomination by the political parties might not be acceptable 'in the light of developments in other parts of the democratic process' and that a body such as the Appointments Commission might need to have an enhanced role in overseeing the process, though quite what that role might be is unclear.

For both types of member, it raises the question of whether terms of appointment should be for life or renewable. Although they could be as long as for life, it says, periods such as three years would fit in with some methods of nomination although this would lose the advantages of independence. In fact, terms of office at the head of professional bodies are often shorter still.

The White Paper lists advantages and disadvantages to a nominated House. The advantages it sees are:

- *Range of representation*: a wider range is possible, including among party representatives

119

- *Independence*: revision of legislation benefits from the involvement of non-politicians
- *Expertise*: including people with significant specialist expertise could enhance its contribution
- *Status*: there would be 'no risk' of endangering the supremacy of the Commons (implying that a body with higher status would do so)
- *Continuity*: claiming that constitutional development in this country has been 'gradual and incremental', continuing with nomination would fall into this category. It might be fairer to say that it would fall into the category of 'no change'. Opinions might differ over the history

Other points are that ex officio members (i.e., the bishops) could remain and that a nominated House would be the cheapest option.

As disadvantages it gives:

- *Question of democracy*: as it says, 'Some will argue that a system which contains no element of election, even indirect election, cannot be democratic or even properly representative of society as a whole.' While this elides the concepts of democracy and representativeness, it cannot be disputed that a democratic body is one whose members have been elected to it
- *Fine-tuning*: attempting to produce a perfect representative body would involve too much interference in the selection process
- *Delegatate*: trying to make the body 'too overtly representative' could turn into its members into delegates

There are a number of important points here although others could have been highlighted. In looking at the appointments system, for example, the issue of patronage and how it is perceived is skirted around, and the question of the time commitments of distinguished appointees is not addressed. Most of the advantages apply more clearly to Crossbenchers than to political members.

From the point of view of the Royal Commission, the more

fundamental questions of fitness for function and the role of the second chamber are not discussed, beyond acknowledging the value of Crossbenchers in revising legislation. The basic question of whether a nominated House would have the legitimacy to fulfil the functions of a second chamber is not addressed by the White Paper, though it will be by us.

Directly elected chamber

The structure of the White Paper changes at this point. Rather than setting out advantages and disadvantages for the next two options, the directly and indirectly elected models, it contains a general discussion of each, but then lists their advantages and disadvantages together, while acknowledging that the extent to which they are shared will vary. The effect is to blur the issues between the two models and this recurs, too, in the general discussion.

Stress is laid on two factors which the White Paper says will assist to decide the 'worth and value' of an elected second chamber, namely its impact on the relationship with the Commons and the context of fundamental change elsewhere in the constitution. Both are clearly key factors in deciding the model to be chosen. To start with the impact on the Commons, however, rather than with whether there should be effective checks and balances on the executive, is to confuse the two bodies. It also obscures the distinction between amending government bills and challenging the pre-eminence of the Commons, promoting the facile assumption that every amendment passed to a government bill is necessarily a challenge to the supremacy of the Commons.

As the White Paper points out, the Labour Government has already introduced new methods of voting for the devolved bodies and European Parliament, and possibly voting reform for the Commons. Where second chambers overseas are elected they often use voting systems which are different from those of the primary chamber, electing on different cycles or with a proportion (usually one-third) facing the voters on each occasion. Phasing of elections reduces the effect of swings in public opinion, making a second chamber more stable and more able to take a long-term view. On the other hand, it claims, any of these variants of system, date or proportion could lead to party conflict between the two chambers and constitutional instability.

Indirectly elected chamber

Turning to the indirectly elected model, the document points out that it can be found in both unitary and federal states (as can the directly elected models). It refers to local authorities for the first time, saying that in other countries members of local councils, regional assemblies and the primary chamber (i.e., MPs) may be part of the electoral college which chooses the second chamber. Then, in spite of their protestations to the contrary, a Government view suddenly emerges:

> With regard to party political members, indirect elections to the future second chamber by bodies with specific local interests could work well alongside a system of UK-wide political appointments.[26]

Together with another key sentence (see page 126), it appears to describe what the Government thinks it wants, and would wish the Royal Commission to recommend. Indirect election, it says, by the devolved institutions, regional chambers and London Assembly would have two advantages. It would 'demonstrate a clear connection' between them and Westminster. It would also mean that 'in many cases' those selecting the members would themselves have been elected. We cannot but observe that precisely the same point can be made of prime-ministerial nomination.

On the first point, as we shall see in the next chapter, giving seats to the devolved institutions might have the opposite effect to that intended. More importantly, many countries (e.g., Australia) see no need to give seats in the second chamber to their sub-national institutions, as opposed sometimes to the populations of those areas. Furthermore, there is no discussion in the White Paper of the different ways in which the objective of strengthening the Union could be achieved.

On the second, the fact that not all of the selectors would themselves be elected people may seem to weaken claims for the democratic content of the indirectly elected model. It arises because of the make-up of the English regional chambers, which are likely to include business representatives and possibly others who are not councillors.

Nor, however, might this be the only, or even the most significant, limitation on the degree to which the indirectly elected model could be seen as democratic. The White Paper suggests that the Royal Commission should consider whether those nominated by the institutions (including those chosen by MEPs) might not need to be members of those bodies.[27] In other words, it would not be MEPs, MSPs or regional councillors who sat in the second chamber but others nominated by them who need not themselves be elected people. At that point, the line between the indirectly elected model and the nominated one would effectively disappear.

Lumping direct and indirect election together, the White Paper again gives a list of advantages and disadvantages.[28] As advantages it offers:

- *Legitimacy*. It says: 'There can be no doubt about the democratic mandate of an elected body. The people, directly or indirectly, would have given their consent to the formation of the whole of their legislature.' Leaving aside the point just made, that neither those selecting nor those chosen will necessarily be elected people, this statement blurs two distinct processes. It assumes that decisions in which the voters participate and others in which they do not can be treated as equivalent. In what sense would a decision to send a businessman in Tyne and Wear (not himself a member of the regional chamber or assembly) to parliament have the consent of the people?

- *Status of members*. Unlike the earlier assessment of the nominated chamber, nothing is said under this heading about the status of the body and the supremacy of the Commons. Instead, the document says that membership of the second chamber would be a job with specific duties. This seems to acknowledge that lack of time could prevent

members of the devolved and regional institutions themselves from carrying out the role.

- *Representation*. All areas and shades of view could be represented. This is obviously more true of direct election than
indirect, where even if those chosen have a mandate, it is
unlikely to cover the whole of their area.

The point is also made, again, that an elected House is more
likely than a nominated body to include younger members,
which does apply to both models. More fundamentally, the
White Paper says that creating an elected second chamber
would be an 'unequivocal sign' that the Government was
committed to bicameralism. This is obviously all the more
true the stronger the body created.

The disadvantages are suggested as:

- *Conflict with the Commons*. The White Paper lays stress on
the electoral system as the key to not creating a body which
could challenge the supremacy of the Commons. Once
again, the obvious point should be noted that challenging
its supremacy would go considerably beyond merely more
frequently exercising its revising function.

Naturally, if a directly elected model were chosen, it would
be fundamental to ensure that the primary chamber remained
supreme. The White Paper rightly warns of an outcome to be
avoided, but it does not identify an inherent disadvantage in
such a model.

- *Loss of independent and ex officio members*. A wholly
elected (or wholly indirectly elected) chamber would make
it 'virtually impossible' to retain Crossbenchers and the
place of ex officio bishops would probably become unsustainable.
- *Transitional difficulties*. The White Paper suggests that the
transition could be most difficult with a House all of which
was elected at the same time. A House elected in tranches
over a longer period would obviously ease this process.
- *Higher costs*. The cost of elections and of salaries for elected

members and research facilities would increase expenditure on the second chamber (although it is unclear whether this would not also apply to a nominated chamber).

Once again, some issues are omitted, such as the role which forms of direct (rather than indirect) election could play in strengthening the representation at the centre of the devolved nations and regions. The core issue here is clearly the legitimacy of the second chamber, the basic reason for its reform. This will, as the White Paper hints but does not say, vary between the directly and indirectly elected models. It portrays the relationship with the Commons in wholly negative terms – the risk of conflict. Achieving a successful reform will rely on getting the balance right between sufficient legitimacy to fulfil the role (and thereby strengthen parliament as a whole) and insufficient legitimacy or power to challenge the supremacy of the Commons.

A mixed chamber

What the White Paper describes as a mixed chamber includes at least two variants: direct election with nomination and indirect election with nomination. (Conceivably all three could be combined although, contrary to press reports before Christmas 1998, this has not found favour with the Government.) The issues differ between them.

Three 'themes' are suggested by the Government against which any form of House should be judged: its legitimacy and fitness for its purpose; its independence; its relationship with the House of Commons. It scores a nominated House highly on the second and third but low on the first. A wholly elected House scores highly on the first and second but not on the third. When it comes to a House based on direct election and nomination, however, the White Paper dodges the issue. It mentions specifically the two-thirds elected, one-third nominated model proposed for the Conservatives by Lord Home's committee in 1978, saying that there is 'nothing peculiarly compelling about that balance'. As to its first and second themes, it is silent. On the third, it says:

Up to two-thirds elected, especially if this were to be directly elected, could in terms of the relationship with the House of Commons share many of the disadvantages of a wholly elected second chamber.[29]

This carefully crafted statement appears to say more than it actually does. In the final chapter of this book, we shall return to this statement, and the Government's three themes, to assess to what extent it is based on fact.

Having said earlier that nomination and indirect election could work well together, the second key sentence appears in the White Paper's closing paragraphs in general terms:

The advantages of the right combination of a nominated and indirectly or directly elected chamber could be significant.[30]

Drawing together what has already been said, it briefly repeats the advantages of a nominated House: independence in scrutiny; interests outside politics; expertise; inclusion of under-represented groups; retention of bishops and law lords; distinctive membership. Advantages of an elected House would be: the legitimacy of an electoral mandate; status; geographical spread of representation; younger members; commitment to two chambers.

A mixed House, it concludes, would combine the best features of the present House with an 'indubitably democratic' method of selection. Whether this description can really be applied to the Government's apparent preference, given the limitations on its democratic nature revealed in the White Paper, is probably a question of more than linguistic taste.

Language matters. Words such as 'elected' and 'democratic' can be stretched in their meaning. The basic choices as to composition lie between three systems: nomination, indirect election and direct election. The second and third are distinct. It is to these basic choices and the options arising from them that we now turn.

Five models for membership

So, following the White Paper, what seem to be the options, fleshed out in a little more detail, for the composition of a second chamber? *Pace* the White Paper's four models, it might be more helpful to look at five. These are purely examples. They are based on what seem to be realistic options in the light of the pointers it contains, particularly towards a mixed House based on nomination and either indirect or direct election[31] (At this point, a wholly indirectly elected House has been left out for this reason.) At the same time, the options listed here treat direct and indirect election separately and distinguish some of the types of mixed House which the White Paper approaches as one model.

These options merely illustrate how the three basic methods of choosing members in the White Paper (direct election, indirect election and nomination) could be combined. It is these three methods and the choices underlying them which form the core of the debate.

The models range, on a democratic spectrum, from the wholly nominated to the wholly elected as follows:

1. Wholly nominated
2. Mixed: nominated and indirectly elected
3. Mixed: indirectly elected, directly elected and nominated
4. Mixed: directly elected and nominated
5. Wholly directly elected

Option 1. Wholly nominated House

This would be a House wholly composed of life peers or members nominated for a term. This model would effectively preserve the status quo after most of the hereditary peers had gone. Those who had remained under the Weatherill amendment would either leave too or be made life peers.

As with the present life peers, political appointees would probably comprise some 75 per cent of the members. Continuing the practice in the transitional House, there would be a share-out of vacancies determined as to numbers by the Prime Minister, probably in the general direction of the parties' proportions of the vote at the preceding general election. An appointments commission would nominate non-political members. Bishops and other faith representatives would be nominated by their Churches and religious groups. Law lords would continue to be nominated by the Prime Minister.

Option 2. Mixed: nominated and indirectly elected

Although the White Paper does not say so in terms, this appears to be the Government's initial preference. Life peers would remain and probably form the majority of the House, perhaps as much as three-quarters. Joining them would be some indirectly elected appointees from the devolved institutions and regional chambers in England (the latter being councillors in the first instance who would be replaced by members of regional assemblies if created in a given area). One press report before the appearance of the White Paper suggested that perhaps 10 per cent of the Scottish Parliament and Welsh Assembly could have seats in a second chamber.[32] Overall, political members would probably form much the same proportion as in the transitional House, with numbers of life peers being shared out in the direction of each party's vote at the preceding election.

Most of the non-political members would continue to be nominated by an appointments commission as in option 1. A few could be named by regional levels of business, the voluntary sector and professional bodies and by universities.

Option 3. Mixed: indirectly elected, directly elected and nominated

Some weeks before the White Paper appeared, this model was reported in the press to be the Government's preferred option. It could be composed of equal thirds of each type. The regional third would be politicians chosen by the devolved institutions or regions as in option 2. The directly elected third could be chosen by a proportional system of voting in

128

regional constituencies. The final third would be mostly independents, probably life peers, again chosen largely by an appointments commission with some regional nominees as in option 2, although some political life peers might also remain to keep the party proportion of the House at about 75 per cent.

Option 4. Mixed: directly elected and nominated

A House in which at least half of the members are directly elected and the remainder are nominated. The elected members could be chosen by a proportional system from regional constituencies, or another system not considered suitable for the House of Commons. The Conservative Home Committee report in 1978 suggested a House which was two-thirds elected and one-third nominated.

The nominated members could be nominated either centrally or regionally as in option 2 or 3, or a mixture of each. The nominated members would ideally be wholly non-political, although a small number might continue to be nominated by the political parties. Subject to this latter point, life peerages would be phased out for political members but future non-political nominees would probably still be life peers.

Option 5. Wholly directly elected

A House in which all the members are directly elected, possibly by the same electoral system as option 4. Life peerages would be phased out. Unlike the other options, there would be no non-political or Crossbench members of this House, and unlike all the other options, the bishops, religious representatives and law lords would have no place. Since it would be a wholly political House, the membership could accordingly be fewer.

A Conservative model
In December 1998, William Hague floated an idea for a different model to the press. It was described in one headline as an elected House, but was in fact another, starker, variant of

the indirectly elected model. Under this plan, the second chamber would be composed of people chosen by MPs, or indirectly elected by some other means, in proportion to the parties' performances at the previous general election. The bizarre result would be two Houses which were identically composed. The second chamber would be under the automatic political control of any government with a majority in the Commons. In the past (or rather, when there have been Labour governments) Conservatives have been highly critical of what Lord Hailsham called the 'elective dictatorship'. Yet this scheme would double it – the second chamber would simply endorse whatever measures were agreed in the Commons. The best that could be said of this chamber would be that it would be unlikely to offend anyone. More likely, it would be viewed as a rubber stamp.

An indication of the public's view, at least before the publication of the White Paper, appeared in a poll conducted by ICM for the *Guardian* newspaper.[33] A weighted sample of 1123 adults was asked what should happen at the second stage of reform. The answers revealed very strong support for the directly democratic options. Asked whether the second chamber should be elected directly by the public, 44 per cent agreed.[34] A slightly smaller proportion (36 per cent) backed a second chamber which was mainly elected by the public but with a minority of members appointed as life peers. (In other words, 80 per cent of those questioned supported options 4 or 5 above.) Only 9 per cent said that the second chamber should be made up of appointed life peers only, and 11 per cent were 'Don't Knows'. The questions did not cover indirectly elected options.

  In the Gallup poll for the *Daily Telegraph*, published on 8 June 1998, the proportions were reversed. Asked to choose as to the broad composition, 52 per cent supported 'a mixture of life peers and elected members' while 44 per cent preferred an 'entirely elected' body. Overall, more than half (52 per cent) favoured an elective element.

CHAPTER FOUR

THE KEY CHOICE

The three methods: nomination, indirect election, direct election

The options for reform are all variants of three basic systems: nomination, indirect election and direct election. The processes of nomination and indirect election overlap and the Government's apparent preference extends this. The three systems have various advantages and disadvantages, depending in some cases on the combination in which they are intended to be used.

Nomination

A nominated House would essentially make permanent the transitional House. It is, of course, the same plan as in 1968/9 with the difference that hereditary peers would then have retained the right to attend and speak – but not to vote – for their lifetime. A chamber which, following the Cranborne deal, would be capped at no more than 650 members would be made up of life peers or term appointees whom the sovereign would appoint.

Political appointments would be at the nomination of the party leaders. The Prime Minister would, as proposed in the White Paper, give up his sole right to advise the Queen, allowing nominations from Opposition party leaders, in effect, to pass direct to the monarch while he retained control only over his own party's names. The allocation could be expected to move in the direction of the proportion of each party's votes at the previous general election, as suggested in Labour's 1997 manifesto, but on the basis that this was a target.

No party would have a majority in the nominated House; Labour would have broad parity with the Conservatives. Assuming that the size of the House was capped, and given the rate of deaths among life peers (about 18 per year in the present House), the number of political vacancies occurring might be only 12–13 per year. In practice, the length of time between elections would probably be insufficient to allow such a balance to be reached. The only way to achieve the balance would be to remove the cap and straight away, after each election, create as many new peers as were necessary to reflect the parties' proportionate strengths. This would be unsustainable since, particularly when power changed hands, it would simply make an already large House continually even larger.[1]

In appointing non-political Crossbenchers, the monarch would be advised by an appointments commission of privy councillors or similar persons. Taking an outgoing approach, the commission might invite suggestions from outside organisations and over time develop this to ensure that a wide range of professions, institutions and voluntary bodies were consulted, including sectors such as education, the arts, industry and agriculture. This could, however, be a slow process unless a large number of the present Crossbenchers were encouraged to 'retire', since in a capped House the panel would only be dealing with replacing those who had died. Crossbench vacancies would probably only arise at the rate of five or six per year.

Bishops from the Church of England would continue to sit in the House, although their numbers might be reduced, and they would be joined by representatives of other faiths. Law lords would probably continue, although their position is highly anomalous as both judges and legislators, and the increasing public visibility of the law lords – especially in the controversy over the links between Lord Hoffmann and Amnesty International in the Pinochet judgement – may cast into question their role as parliamentarians. Their appointments, while formally made by the Queen, arise on the advice of the Prime Minister and that of the Lord Chancellor. The position of the latter represents perhaps an even greater anomaly. As head of the judiciary, Speaker of the House of Lords and a senior government minister, the Lord Chancellor straddles courts, government and parliament like no other figure, mainly for historical reasons. The creation of a permanent appointed House would almost certainly expose the extent of this position to closer scrutiny.

The present Crossbench/independent life peers number 129 and comprise about a quarter of the total. This percentage would probably remain broadly the same. In theory, it could be suggested that non-politicians should form a higher proportion than at present, or even the majority of a new House. While there might be scope for independents to form up to one-third of the chamber, above that level the political nature of the process would be compromised.

A House of experts

The Left flirted briefly in the 1930s with a non-political and wholly nominated second chamber, sometimes known as the House of Industry. The fashion was for élites, and Mosley and others expressed interest in a chamber which would bring together the major interests in society. Its popularity did not last long: so-called 'corporatist' decision-making became closely associated with fascist systems of government. There is perhaps an echo of this approach in the White Paper where it mentions the phrase 'functional constituencies' to describe the possibility of structuring representation through professions, trades and interests. It also mentions the controversy over these before the handover of Hong Kong.

There is no rationale for placing parliamentary responsibilities wholly in the hands of expert individuals. The second chamber would be remote from public opinion and wholly unaccountable. The government of the day would have little overt influence in it since the debate would be largely conducted in non-political terms. On the other hand, it would be dominant. Lacking the legitimacy to use any powers it might possess, the second chamber could only have a commenting and advisory role. Questions of principle, and political problems in detail, would be passed by default or through a lack of political organisation. The second chamber would be unable to carry out its functions effectively, worsening the present situation rather than improving it.

Nomination and the Royal Commission

It is, of course, striking that the Royal Commission has been asked to consider a purely nominated House at all. While there is obviously no objection on the ground of examining all the issues thoroughly, the White Paper expressed an apparent preference for a more mixed model. As we have seen, however, the Prime Minister's earlier commitment was to 'a more democratically-elected second chamber'. Shortly before the White Paper was published, the Home Secretary, Jack Straw, had said that the Government would make clear its desire for 'a more representative and democratic chamber'.[2] Whether, in light of statements such as these, it is politically conceivable that the Royal Commission could be persuaded to recommend retaining a wholly nominated House – or even if it did, whether it would be politically acceptable for any party to support it – remains to be seen.

Advantages and disadvantages

Continuity and difference
The possible advantages of a nominated House might begin with continuity, drawing on what is often seen as an evolutionary approach to constitutional change in this country. There could be some pragmatic advantage in drawing on the experience of the present life peers and enabling the House to continue its work without disruption. Whether this would qualify in itself as an argument for a wholly nominated House would depend on how far that experience could be deployed under other models too. While continuity may have played its

part in developing our constitution, some of the largest steps such as the Great Reform Act or the Bill of Rights have been anything but evolutionary. Nor has this consideration commended itself to the Government in other areas of its constitutional programme, such as devolution in Scotland and Wales.

No one could argue that a wholly nominated House would be a copy of the House of Commons. Its membership would be wholly distinct and would underline the supremacy of the Commons. This is an important point, but again would apply to every model except a second chamber which was wholly directly elected on the same basis as the Commons.

Range of representation
The main argument for nomination is the possible range of representation in the second chamber. Experts and representatives who have something to offer to public policy-making, but who have no political platform – or even aptitude for politics – can be accommodated within an essentially political process in order to revise and to deliberate.

The problem is that the argument stops there. Used to support the case for a wholly – as opposed to a partially – nominated body, it is flawed, because, as emerges from a reading of the White Paper, it applies mainly to the Crossbenches. Although it can reasonably be argued that non-party peers appointed for their expertise may 'represent' their field, at least in a general sense, barring the occasional exception, this does not apply to the party peers. Yet it is they who would form the majority of the House. Political peers may bring a wealth of experience, but they sit as party supporters, owing their position to their political affiliation and representing no one but themselves. Representativeness cannot be a rationale if it applies to just a quarter of the members. Indeed, emphasising the claims of the Crossbench minority to be representative undermines the legitimacy of the political peers who form the majority.

Independence
It is claimed that life peers are independent because they

answer to no one and cannot be removed. This mirrors the argument that hereditary peers are independent; and then takes it a stage further by adding that life peers have been appointed on their own merits. It is the opposite of the Conservative view that a House of life peers would be over-compliant. In fact, the argument for life peers' independence is unproven; or, to put it more kindly, their intrinsic independence is perhaps still latent. To the relief of the party whips, the division records show that, the odd maverick apart, political life peers are at least as likely as their hereditary counterparts to follow their party line.

The argument can be taken in its own terms but turned on its head. If they were completely independent, would this necessarily be an advantage? The government would have great difficulty is securing its legislation or organising its business. What is surely required from a second chamber is wisdom, allied to political reality, and a sense of what is publicly acceptable. A House which was fully independent might well prove wholly out of touch with, and unresponsive to, public opinion.

The point about what the public finds acceptable is important. A second chamber which followed every fashion would be useless. Just as valueless, however, would be a second chamber which refused, or was unable, to take public feeling into account in reaching its decisions. There is much nonsense talked by opponents of reform about the innate value of independence; what matters is how it is exercised. The occasions when the independence of the present House has struck a chord have been when it is expressing public opinion, not when it has flouted it. Moreover, in a mature democracy, the quality of public policy-making depends on a healthy interaction between public opinion and parliamentary representatives, who are accountable at the ballot box but free, in the meantime, to exercise their judgement. It does not depend on some non-political trait of independence, which at times seems almost to mask an atavistic fear of the electorate or the political process. The reintroduction of hanging for murder, for example, is denied to a public which wants it not by independently minded peers but by MPs who consistently vote it

136

down regardless of opinion polls.

Whatever the value of the argument about independence, we should not forget that only life peers have an assured tenure and might thus be expected to show more independence than term appointees who might wish to be reappointed.

Cost

The final argument made in favour of a wholly nominated House is that is would cost less. It may be true that it would be less likely than the other models to exceed significantly the cost of the present House of Lords (£40 million in 1997/8, or £37,000 per member per annum), although it need not be the case that members would remain unsalaried, for example. Were the future second chamber to prove more expensive to run, there would clearly be some opportunity cost in another area of expenditure. The reality, however, is that it is a second-order issue, particularly at the sort of level of spending likely to be contemplated. It would be difficult to imagine a proposed reform which increased the democratic workings of the House of Commons being resisted *in principle* on the grounds of cost. As a comparison, the House of Commons cost £241 million in 1997/8, a modest sum. Given that benchmark, it can be seen that the cost implications of reforms of the Lords are not such that they need constitute a primary issue.

Legitimacy and patronage

If the arguments in favour are mixed, there are a number of straightforward arguments against a wholly nominated House. The charge that a permanent nominated House would institutionalise patronage is difficult to ignore. While the cruder objections can be dispelled by the creation of an appointments commission, the dropping of the Prime Minister's power to decide nominations from other parties and a cap on the numbers, this does not remove the fact that someone other than the electorate decides, whether it is the party leaders or the commission. A reform along these lines extends patronage from about half of the House to the whole of it.

The qualifications expected of an appointee would come under scrutiny, with the likelihood that in practice a higher standard would apply to independents appointed for their expertise than to political members appointed for their politics. This would be a serious development which would do nothing for the standing of the second chamber. The question of who would determine these qualifications, how they were judged and whether appointees had lived up to them would all become matters of public comment; as would the issue of whether, and if so how (and by whom), an appointee later found wanting might be removed.

The composition of a permanently appointed House might, over time, come to be seen as less legitimate than that of the present House. While outnumbered by hereditary peers, life peers have been able to appear comparatively more legitimate, but this perception could change – particularly for political peers – if the transitional House were to prove more than strictly temporary.

Time

The volume of business in the Lords rises consistently and has shown no sign of diminishing as the Labour Government has forged ahead with its manifesto bills. It is important to be realistic about the limitations placed by time on the pool of people available for nomination. In practice, a nominated House – at least if it remains unsalaried – will always tend to be older.

Political appointees will mostly have retired from their former activities. Labour tried to counteract this after the 1997 election, recruiting as peers a younger group in their forties and fifties who are making a second career of membership. Unlike MPs, many have to earn a living outside as well as attending the House, to which are often added the pressures of supporting a second home in the capital, separation from family and friends and extra travelling, sometimes to distant locations. These are familiar to any MP with a seat outside London. Many initially found the demands a great strain, reflected in some cases in their voting records, with the employment pressures eased only for those who have progressed to salaried positions on the Government frontbench. From experience, it should not be assumed that a majority of the political backbenchers in a nominated House would be of working age.

So far as the Crossbenches are concerned, some might be beguiled by the thought of those benches staffed in future by the leaders of their professions, the captains of industry or the leading lights of the voluntary sector. Such people are simply too busy fulfilling those roles to be able to spend the majority of the working week at Westminster, even assuming they wished to give up their professional prospects to do so. Active practitioners in a field would have to come from the respected second rank with fewer commitments. Otherwise, as now, the best of those available would be retired or winding down other commitments.

Whether the House is older or its members still active within their profession matters hardly at all where the nominated element is not the whole of the House; where their contribution is not its main rationale. In a partly elected House, for example, provided the Crossbenches 'add value' to the political debate, it matters less whether they are retired or still professionally active. In a fully nominated House, however, the issue could become whether or not the public felt confidence in the calibre of the people appointed and their work.

Élites and delegates

Creating a permanently nominated House could amount to swapping rule by one élite for that of another. By definition, life peers have already achieved some position, whether in an expert field or through their political activity. For many people at all levels, but especially those in poverty, the unemployed, ethnic minorities and many women, there is no reason why they should consider that life peers represent them and their interests. As people in those positions will say, the only way they consider that someone represents them is if they have elected them, which gives the disadvantaged private citizen a claim on their attention whatever the differences in their respective standing.

The impression of an élite House could be reinforced if, as

is sometimes suggested, the holders of certain positions in society (such as the Chief of the Defence Staff) acquired the status of ex-officio members. The same would be true if some outside organisations were given a right in effect to nominate. People appointed in this way would become delegates from their organisation or policy community, speaking and voting as expected – or even directed – rather than exercising an independent judgement. This would be a serious development in a parliamentary system, and it would be exacerbated further if term appointments, at least other than for long periods, were introduced.

While the danger would be greatest with ex-officio members, considerable care would be needed to prevent other non-party nominees from being treated as delegates – or from seeing themselves in this role. At present, Crossbench and independent life peers are generally appointed in honour of their past endeavours. If the basis were to change so that they were nominated for their future endeavours, it should be made clear that those nominating them, or others in their field, would be in no position to tie their hands. Members attending parliament as spokespeople for a given interest, with a prepared line and a mandate on how to vote, would raise serious implications for the representative nature of Westminster democracy as a whole. Since the Bill of Rights 1689, rules of parliamentary 'privilege' have protected both Houses from outside interference in their proceedings and the freedom of speech of members. Cases brought before the Committee of Privileges in the Commons have shown the sensitivities. A vote by a trade union region, for example, that its sponsored MPs should not vote contrary to union policy was a breach of privilege.[3]

The difficulty might be less that professional and other bodies would be unwilling to toe this line – although they might easily infringe it unwittingly – than that, in the absence of any other rationale for their membership, the members concerned would wish to reassure themselves that they were faithfully representing the best opinions in their profession or area of activity. There could further be the risk that members would feel welcome to participate only in debates and divisions covering their own area. To an extent this happens now, although it is muffled by the participation both of political peers and of those Crossbenchers who come regularly. In a wholly nominated House it could become much more significant. If the membership contained, for example, five doctors, their attendance and voting records in their field would be far more noticeable and the subject of public comment than at present. While their interventions on health issues might be influential – and occasionally troublesome to government – their enthusiastic participation in questions of defence policy might be less well received. A more professionalised House, in this narrow sense, might too easily become fragmented and disorganised, holding well-informed but highly specialised debates involving a handful of experts in a dialogue between interest groups, but all too easily leaving the government of the day to pursue its political objectives by default.

The weakest option

Overall, a wholly nominated House would be the weakest of the options. While it would have more legitimacy than the present chamber, it would have no democratic legitimacy by comparison with the House of Commons, and could consequently be largely ineffective. The findings of the Constitution Unit in respect of the Canadian Senate point strongly to this danger.[4]

For that reason, of course, it could be expected to be institutionally attractive to governments. Although probably having no majority, the government of the day could expect to be the largest party, and the votes of some Crossbenchers would probably see it through most divisions. Where a government did lose, it could – as now – overturn the result on the automatic ground that the composition of the second chamber was undemocratic and carried no legitimacy on political questions.

There is a trade-off between legitimacy and powers. To give a nominated House some credibility as a revising chamber, it would need to have fairly extensive formal powers. The result, however, would repeat the situation in both the present House of Lords and the appointed Canadian Senate, whereby a body with little legitimacy was again prevented from using its powers and from performing its proper function.

There may be some, even in Government, who hope that, notwithstanding the political realities, the Royal Commission reports in favour of a version of the transitional House. Political expectations have almost certainly moved too far for this to be feasible, even if it were desirable. Furthermore, the Liberal Democrats would be wholly opposed to it and the Conservatives would regard it as proving their main charge about the Government's intentions.

The democratic arguments are buttressed by the basic reason for reform: because of its lack of legitimacy, the second chamber has been unable for nearly a century to function as it should. To create another body with the same problem would simply replicate the existing imbalance – not between the Commons and Lords, but between parliament and the executive.

Indirect election

Objectives

Options 2 and 3, the indirectly elected models, might be said to offer a counterbalance to devolution and regionalism by applying some constitutional 'glue' to the United Kingdom. The White Paper has complicated this picture by including the proposal that people other than elected members of the devolved institutions and regions could be chosen for the second chamber. We shall examine the concept of 'glue' and whether indirect election is the best way to achieve it. If councillors or elected mayors were to be included, a second claim could be that indirect election could provide a spur to the revival of local government.

Supporters of first-past-the-post in elections to the Commons may also have a third and more tactical objective: to promote a very limited degree of indirect election in the second chamber in a joint referendum as an alternative to electoral reform for the House of Commons – a position which some Conservatives might support. Sceptics might even divine a fourth objective: to produce a chamber whose legitimacy was still weak.

As objectives, there are obvious attractions to binding in the devolved nations and regions, and rebuilding local government. The Home Secretary, Jack Straw, has said of decentralisation under Labour: 'The more powers are devolved to parts of Britain and to citizens, the greater the need for a small, strong centre.'[5]

Irrespective of devolution, a second chamber with legitimacy and powers should be an integral part of that strong centre in its own right.

Constitutional glue

The 'post-devolution' argument is that the nations and regions should themselves be represented in the second chamber to give them a voice at the centre. It is a striking proposal, imposing an overall if asymmetrical pattern on a decentralised structure and offering an identity to the second chamber. There are, however, a number of issues which the Royal Commission will have to address.

The first question is whether the UK should begin to take on aspects of a federal structure as a by-product of redesigning the second chamber. The early United States constitution provided for two members of each state legislature to sit in the federal Senate, while the members of the House of Representatives were directly elected by the people. (Now, of course, US senators are also directly elected.) The USA is a federal country. There may be reasons ultimately to move in that direction in the UK, including the long-term implications of devolution or the future effects of EU membership and the euro. The directions of these questions may evolve over decades. If they come about it should be as considered constitutional developments in their own right.

We should be careful, too, about changing the structure of devolution in ways which could be interpreted as rewriting it; for example, by appearing to reintroduce an element of bicameralism for matters devolved to Edinburgh and Cardiff by giving members of those bodies a dual role. Nor might giving seats in the second chamber to members of the devolved bodies necessarily be the best way of giving the Union a more stable foundation. In the context of the continuing campaign for Scottish independence what, for example, might happen if a separatist party were to win a majority and then refused to take up its seats in the second chamber? In that situation, might not making the devolved bodies the channel for representation have weakened rather than strengthened the Union? The wiser course might be to assess these questions of the fundamental structure of the country separately and in the light of experience.

Reviving local government

Although the White Paper barely mentions it, proposals could emerge from the Royal Commission for local government to provide members for the second chamber. The revival of local government is urgently needed and the introduction of elected mayors will play an important part in that process. One idea which has occasionally been canvassed is for some elected mayors, when created, to have seats. A proposal to allocate seats to mayors in the second chamber could be seen as strengthening the constitutional status of local government and raising its profile in national politics. The presence of local government in the second chamber might be thought to offer some defence against its role being reduced as during the Thatcher/Major era. On the other hand, many present members of the House in all parties have local government experience, but when it came to a division the deciding factor was the party whip. (English regional members could also be councillors from local government in the period before regional assemblies were created.)

Local government should be revived for itself and for what it can give to local communities. Using it as a source of members for a second chamber could distract from that objective, or even harm it. It needs two things: the re-creation of proper powers and autonomy from Whitehall; and sufficient control over its finances so that councils can make their own decisions and defend themselves to their voters. The Government is moving forward on both, through proposals in the Local

Government Bill on local authority capping and 'best value' in local services, and in its White Paper proposals for elected mayors or cabinet systems, new powers and duties to promote the well-being of areas and local partnerships and powers to vary business rates.[6]

Distraction could come if directly elected mayors were put into the second chamber. These new mayors, when introduced, are to be responsible for running the authority, their fellow councillors moving from sharing executive responsibility on committees into more of a backbench scrutiny role. Restricting any local government places to these new figures would obviously be intended to encourage reluctant council leaders down that route. If places were made available only to a minority, such as mayors from the larger authorities and big cities, this could lead to tension between 'old' and 'new' local government and cut across efforts to revive it as a whole.

Local government's main political weakness is the low level of turnout at local elections. Moving to elected mayors might make a significant difference by personalising the issues, but putting them into parliament could complicate the experiment, at least in its early years. If turnout increased in an area eligible to send the mayor to the second chamber, this might be attributed to the contest having been a parliamentary one, rather than because of increased interest in local affairs. On the other hand, if turnout remained flat, mayors could have a poor standing within the second chamber. The revival of local government could also be harmed if mayors or other councillors sent to the second chamber simply became overloaded. We have seen already how some peers face an awkward balance of membership and outside employment. It is very difficult to see how a full-time salaried mayor, other than perhaps one based in London, could manage to do justice both to running a multi-million-pound political organisation and to serving in a revising chamber three or four days each week. From local government's point of view, mayors who fail to make an impact, whether at home or at Westminster, would simply weaken its position further.

Representation in parliament is unlikely to prove the panacea which would strengthen local councils. The pressures

145

of party loyalty, the limited opportunities to participate and the difficulties associated with speaking from a known standpoint could all reduce the impact of members sent from local authorities. Local government is by its nature in a position of constant negotiation and consultation with the government over the implementation of policy. So far as possible, it seeks to conduct the discussion on an all-party basis. If its leaders were also in parliament, their need to obey the whip could cut across these negotiating positions, blunting their ability to negotiate behind the scenes with ministers of their own party. Being obliged to take a public stance could also limit their flexibility to work across party within local government. Equally, if the leaders were too busy to serve in the second chamber, their activities could be undermined by less senior representatives toeing the government and Opposition lines. The relationship with the government could be further complicated by swings in council elections. If, as often happens, these went against the party in power nationally, the result could be local government leaders nightly opposing the government in the division lobbies. If this proposal is made, local authorities might care to consider the possibility that formal representation in parliament, far from elevating their status or insulating them from unfavourable measures, could instead bind them to an uncomfortable degree into the political positions of the government and Opposition parties at Westminster.

English regions

There has for many years been strong support in some parts of the country, notably in the North and parts of the Midlands, for the creation of regional assemblies to give those areas a stronger voice and to focus on increased investment. Ministers see these assemblies as concerned with industrial policy, planning, the development of industrial areas and the revival of rural economies.[7] The Government has legislated for regional development agencies in England, which are to promote economic development from spring 1999. Before assemblies are created, local councillors may be brought together informally in forums known as 'regional chambers'.

The approach is evolutionary. Even when legislation has been enacted, assemblies will only be created where there is local support in a referendum. The Deputy Prime Minister, John Prescott, has stated that no assemblies will be created before 2001/2. It is possible that in some regions they may never be established. In the meantime, the White Paper suggests that regional chambers could be involved in nominating councillors to the second chamber.

It is argued that representing the nascent regions in the second chamber could give them a strong voice at the centre. It would appear to give regional leaders a platform in parliament, offer regions a degree of national visibility and confer extra credibility on the new assemblies in their own areas. As with local government, these would appear, at first sight, to be clear attractions.

Yet from regional government's point of view, many of the same difficulties might apply as with local government. Their relations with central government – crucial to bodies concerned with their share of public grants – might not be assisted by its representatives taking a role in national politics. Seats in the second chamber would be unlikely to give them the voice they anticipated; most parliamentary business would fall outside their assemblies' range of functions. Their primary role would be that of party supporter not regional spokesman. Since the Government has not suggested that the nominating bodies should follow the German example and send representatives solely from the ruling or coalition group, the members would be mixed, presumably in proportion to their parties' local shares of the seats. Just as they would be permanently in political contention in their home area, so they would sit and act in their different party groups in the second chamber, with little opportunity and certainly no encouragement to work together as regional representatives.

The political constraints, as well as the time commitments involved, would be unlikely to appeal to leaders or senior figures in the assembly. Nor would the second chamber necessarily provide much of a forum for promoting the needs of the region. The Maastricht Treaty created a Committee of the Regions to involve regions and local authorities in the EU. As its UK members would recognise, special pleading for the home area would be 'out' in the second chamber; all the more since its main role was revising legislation, with no financial powers and neither a locus nor much interest in government spending in the regions. Indeed, it would be understandable if regional MPs, who privately might not always welcome the presence at Westminster of powerful figures from their own backyard, felt usurped were it to do so. Regional representatives, like other nominees, would need to exercise great care not to be seen as delegates acting on political instructions from their assemblies, whose views could then be discounted by the rest of the second chamber. Instead of using the second chamber to mount a distinctive case for their area, they would be more likely to find their energies and profile becoming submerged in the daily round of a parliamentary backbencher.

The status of the indirect representative

The bugbear of the indirectly elected nominee would be their dual status, whether they were from the local, regional or devolved tiers. Neither fish nor fowl, they would be neither full parliamentarians nor normal members of their own body. Their interests and their answerability would start from a different frame of reference from that of a directly elected member. That person could point to a mandate and an electorate; when they scrutinised legislation or questioned ministers, they would do so from the standpoint of their area and its voters. For their indirectly elected colleague, there would always be the uncertainty of which 'hat' was being worn. A non-elected person chosen by a region or devolved institution as their representative would be in an even weaker position.

Tinkering with devolution

In Scotland, Northern Ireland and Wales, devolved legislation is to be handled by a single chamber rather than by two as at Westminster. There is a necessary asymmetry in, for example, the respective issues which Scottish and English MPs may decide: the famous West Lothian question. The same asymmetry will apply in the second chamber, so that Scottish members of it will be able to discuss English matters which north of the border are reserved for the Edinburgh parliament. Placing MSPs in the second chamber could reopen sensitive questions. The difference between Scottish MPs and their counterparts at Holyrood is that the former have been elected to legislate and scrutinise over the whole range of the UK parliament, whereas members of the Scottish parliament will have been elected to legislate for devolved matters only. We shall return to the implications of basing accountability for broad functions on that of narrower ones, but the point in the context of devolution is that to mix the memberships could produce an unnecessary distraction. The intricacies of devolution are such that there might be wisdom in not reinvigorating arguments over powers (or whether there should have been a Scottish second chamber) by bringing MSPs and other devolved members to Westminster who could have a wider remit than English MPs.

One other matter of devolution is relevant here. William Hague has suggested that devolution may lead in the future to an English parliament. Were this to be created in the future, it too might expect to be represented in the second chamber. In those circumstances, both English MPs and members of the devolved parliament might find themselves elected to bodies concerned with the same range of responsibilities, unlike their Scottish, Welsh and Northern Irish counterparts. Would English members of the UK parliament find this a comfortable arrangement? The Government's alternative has been to reintroduce a Commons committee to discuss regional issues.[8] This approach will doubtless go a long way to dealing with some of these issues.

Five questions on indirect election

Indirect election as a system is inherently unsatisfactory. The Lords' (and Labour's) greatest victory over Mrs Thatcher was when they defeated precisely such bodies in the GLC/metropolitan counties paving bill. Five questions can be asked in weighing up whether it should have a place in the second chamber.

1. Are direct and indirect election equivalent?

The concept of direct election is familiar. Those directly elected to a body hold their seats in it by decision of the voters. They have a duty to represent the electors in their constituency to the best of their ability, whether or not those electors voted for them. At the next election, if they stand again they will be judged at least partly on their past performance. Between polls, electors may complain if they consider a representative's behaviour to be unsatisfactory.

In contrast, indirectly elected members of a body hold their seats in it by a decision not of the electorate but of another (usually lower) body. The members are certainly directly elected, but to another body than the one in question. It is the other body (or often groups of them) who have the right to make appointments to the forum concerned and have chosen these representatives from among their own members to fill the seats. The representatives are accountable to the body or grouping which appointed them. It is the other members who appointed them, rather than either the voters who elected them to their seat or the electorate for the larger area, who judge their performance and may complain in the meantime.

There are rival tests here. Those who claim that the two types are equivalent rely on the elected status of each. People who have been elected to something, it is said, are different from those who have not; both directly and indirectly elected persons have the endorsement of the electorate, draw a mandate from them and have a constituency to consult when issues arise. Thus, it is claimed, a second chamber of indirectly elected members can properly be described as 'elected'. On that basis, local government bodies such as the West Midlands Passenger Transport Authority or the London Grants Committee are to be regarded as elected.

The opposite view is simpler: the electors have not voted for those members to carry out the responsibilities which they now exercise and so they have no mandate from them for what they do. In addition, the second chamber is concerned with a far wider range of issues than would fall within the responsibilities of the nominating bodies and so it could not claim its legitimacy from their elections.

This second view focuses not on the status of the members as individuals, but on their lines of accountability. The members of an indirectly elected body are accountable to the bodies which placed them there; in a conflict, they will be judged on what they have done for that body. Reporting back and consultation will be to the appointing body, not to the electorate. It is not clear what the body could do with the report, and still more so if the representative were not one of its members. Furthermore, any redress for electors will have to be provided by the nominating body rather than directly. Most people will in any case have no electoral link with the member in question since that person will sit for somewhere other than their individual constituency or area.

2. *Should one person do two jobs?*

As we saw in looking at the nominated House and at elected mayors, there is the practical question of whether people can realistically be expected to undertake two jobs at once, usually with a considerable distance between them. This has no doubt led to the Government's proposal that others outside the devolved bodies and regional assemblies could be chosen as their representatives. In the German upper house, for example, this problem is resolved by officials sitting in for the politicians; a solution unlikely to be acceptable in the Westminster parliament. As we have also seen, the members sent from devolved, regional or possibly local bodies are unlikely to be drawn from their current leaderships. They may instead be the loyal backbencher, the frontbencher who lacks a role or the rival whom it is politically convenient to remove to London.

Although time is the main issue, it is also worth pointing out that the jobs of scrutinising government and running a large organisation such as a region or local authority are not the same and make different demands. Many MPs who come from local authorities miss the challenge of taking decisions and seeing a result on the ground; legislative scrutiny is rarely glamorous and still more will that be true of the second chamber.

3. Is there a risk of creating delegates?

In practice, the appointing body may be in a position to exercise quite detailed supervision of the activities of its members. Even more than members nominated by outside organisations, there is a clear risk of their being made delegates by the political bodies which send them, and this would cut across the nature of parliamentary representation. Nor might this be restricted to political nominees. Non-political appointments from regional groupings of business, the voluntary sector or professional bodies could be subject to intense monitoring and supervision, all the more intense since it would be conducted in private. As with members in a wholly nominated House, systems of accountability back to the nominating bodies, however politically desirable, might in fact raise difficult issues of parliamentary privilege. Moreover, the members might prove unwilling to contribute on subjects outside the responsibility of their nominating body.

4. Is there an accountability gap?

By definition, parliament may discuss anything. So, even allowing for areas such as public finance remaining reserved to the Commons, the second chamber will deal with a vastly greater range of matters than the nominating bodies, probably encompassing most areas of public policy. There is no 'democratic' rationale, for example, for a regional councillor to have a vote on defence policy, if they have a place, or a local councillor to be able to quiz ministers on the courts and legal system, since neither was elected for that purpose.

Even if one could be devised, those members would still have major gaps in their accountability. There would be no one to whom they could validly report many of their activities. As a result, they would be subject to no accountability of any kind in those areas. The size of the accountability gap would vary. Those from bodies with wider responsibilities would have greater accountability. Those from bodies with the narrowest, either the English regions or local authorities, would have the least. In those cases, most activities in the following departmental areas would fall into the gap:

> Foreign Office; Treasury; Defence; most of the Home Office; Trade and Industry; Social Security; Health; Agriculture, Fisheries and Food; part of Employment; most of Culture, Media and Sport; International Development; part of Transport and the natural environment; UK aspects of Scotland, Wales and Northern Ireland matters; Lord Chancellor's Department.

The result would be an appearance of accountability where in practice it did not exist. The gap could be closed by limiting the indirect representatives to their own subject areas, but this would weaken the second chamber unacceptably by introducing distinctions among its members and limiting its scope.

5. Should different members and electoral cycles be mixed?
If directly and indirectly elected members were both in the second chamber, the former would be seen as having the higher status. There could be similar perceived differences as between members of the devolved bodies, regional assembly members and (if included) local councillors. While they would sit as political colleagues, the disparities could lead to strain. How likely is it, for example, that directly elected politicians would consent to be led by an indirectly elected nominee?

The differing electoral cycles of the various nominating bodies are a factor which the Royal Commission might wish to take into account. The Northern Ireland Assembly was elected in 1998 (although it is hoped it will take over its full responsibilities from 1999) while Scotland and Wales are on four-year cycles from that year. English regions would have to be delayed until May 2003 to join the same cycle, while the London Assembly is planned to run from May 2000. There are local government elections in most years and many councils already face election in three years out of four. The Government wishes to move to more frequent elections still, so that more areas would vote every year.[9] The practical consequence of a second chamber of this type is that the membership could be subject to constant change. While it might be thought to offer an up-to-date reflection of public opinion, it would have little cohesion in its membership.

It is clear that an indirectly elected body is qualitatively different from a body whose members are directly elected. The Royal Commission will need to examine all these issues: the relative status of the two types; whether members would have the time to fulfil the role; whether there is an accountability gap (and, if so, whether it matters); and whether types of members and mandates should be mixed. It would need to look at the timing of change and whether making reform of the second chamber dependent on other changes yet to be introduced is valid, or risks losing momentum on Lords reform once again; and, more fundamentally, whether direct representation of elected and unelected bodies, rather than the people themselves, is desirable or likely to contribute to the stability of devolution.

While an indirectly elected model would not produce a House as weak as a nominated one, its members would still lack the standing of those who can point to direct electoral accountability for the job they are doing. The same dilemma could apply as in the case of the wholly nominated House: whether or not to accord powers which were too strong to a House which was too weak.

The core questions are whether direct election is more appropriate to legislative revision, what the identity of the House should be and, crucially, whether an elected membership would confer sufficient legitimacy to enable it to fulfil its functions while preserving the superiority of the House of Commons. It is to those issues that we now turn.

Direct election

The basis of options 4 and 5 is a House which is directly elected, the final option being based on the pure principle. Option 5 would produce a wholly elected bicameral parliament of the kind taken for granted in many other countries. Although largely resting on the principle of direct election, option 4 (a House partly elected and partly nominated) represents a compromise. We shall return to this option at the start of the next chapter. For the moment, the issue is the principle of direct election as represented by option 5 and its suitability for a second chamber.

Methods of election

It is generally agreed that any democratic element in the second chamber should be elected on a different basis from that of the House of Commons. To use the same electoral system would almost certainly lead to rivalry and undermine the basis of the superiority of the Commons.

It has also become generally accepted that the defining feature of the present electoral system for the House of Commons is the constituency link between members and electors grouped into individual voting areas. This produces accountability of a very direct nature. MPs know their areas and many of their constituents well, are themselves well known in their communities and can, in consequence, rightly claim to be closely in touch with local opinion. Most see dozens of their constituents every week and are in constant touch with their local party supporters. They are highly visible in their areas, their activities being regularly reported by local press and broadcasters. They are in a position, where appropriate, to draw highly localised issues to the attention of the House of Commons, or to use them as examples to advance a point of view. MPs survey the issues passing before them with a keen appreciation of the impact on their local constituency. This direct democratic link, which works in both directions, gives the House of Commons a unique legitimacy in addition to its status as the only directly elected chamber. The voter has a direct means of access to the executive. To remove it would alter substantially the character of British politics.

For this reason, the Independent Commission on the voting system (the Jenkins Commission) has recommended the Alternative Vote Top Up system as a possible replacement for first-past-the-post for the House of Commons. The terms of reference of the Commission required it to take into account the 'maintenance of a link between MPs and geographical constituencies'. AV Top Up incorporates some 15–20 per cent of additional members chosen according to the proportion of the vote achieved by each party in local top-up areas. But the basis of the recommendation is that while it is a more proportional system, the main electoral unit is that of the individual constituency.

On the same basis, there is wide agreement on the part of other studies into Lords reform that not only should the system differ from that of the Commons, and that the latter should remain constituency-based, but that the units of representation for elections to the second chamber should be the English regions, Scotland, Wales and Northern Ireland. The Conservative committee which reported under the late Lord Home of the Hirsel in 1978 recommended proportional representation, possibly using regional lists. The Labour working party on electoral systems chaired by Lord Plant of Highfield which submitted its main report in 1993, and a report by Jeremy Mitchell and Anne Davies published by the Labour-leaning Institute of Public Policy Research (IPPR) in the same year[10] both recommended what is known as the regional list system. Regionally based electoral systems for the second chamber are the policy of both the Liberal Democrats and Charter 88, the constitutional reform pressure group. The independent constitutional research body, the Constitution Unit, took no position in analysing the options in 1996, but in its description of possible electoral systems pointed only to regional models.

The Plant Committee examined the possible electoral systems for the second chamber. These may be summarised as follows:[11]

- *First-past-the-post (or simple plurality system)*: the candidate receiving the highest number of votes in a constituency is elected. This is of course the system used for the House of Commons and local government elections (apart from the London Assembly and mayor).

- *Second ballot*: in the first round, only a candidate receiving more than 50 per cent is elected. For a second round, only

156

some candidates go forward (either a certain number or those above a certain percentage of the vote). The result is then determined by first-past-the-post.

- *Alternative Vote*: voters in a single-member constituency rank the candidates. Only a candidate gaining over 50 per cent is elected outright. Otherwise, second preferences of lower-placed candidates (starting with the lowest) are transferred until one candidate has a majority.

- *Supplementary Vote*: unlike the Alternative Vote, the voter marks only a first and second preference. A candidate with over 50 per cent is elected. Otherwise, all but the first two are eliminated and the second preferences from the other candidates are added to their totals. To be used for the London mayor.

- *List systems*: in multi-member constituencies or regions, electors vote for a party list rather than an individual candidate. The seats are apportioned between the parties according to their share of the vote. Individuals are elected according to their ranking on their party's list. Some variants allow electors to alter the ranking of individuals on the list (the so-called 'open' as opposed to 'closed' lists). This applies from June 1999 to the European Parliament (except Northern Ireland).

- *Additional Member system (or Mixed Member system)*: electors cast two votes – for a candidate and a party. Some members are elected on a first-past-the-post basis in single-member constituencies; others from a party list against which seats are allocated to achieve proportional representation (e.g., over a region). The proportion of seats between constituency and top-up members may vary. Applies from May 1999 to the Scottish Parliament and Welsh Assembly and will be used for the London Assembly.

- *Single Transferable Vote*: in multi-member constituencies, voters rank candidates in order of preference. Where a candidate exceeds a quota for election, his or her votes above the quota are redistributed to the second preference. If no one reaches the quota, the lowest candidate drops out and

157

his or her second preferences are redistributed. Redistribution continues until the required number passes the quota and is elected. This is used in Northern Ireland for elections to the European Parliament and Assembly.

The first four systems are based on single-member constituencies and can be rejected for the second chamber for this reason.

Additional Member systems can also be ruled out for this purpose, particularly where – as for the devolved bodies – most of the seats are constituency-based. In Scotland, 73 of the 129 seats in the Parliament are elected from the same constituencies as the House of Commons (except for the separation of Orkney and Shetland) and the remaining 56 seats are 'topped up' on the basis of seven for each of the eight European constituencies. In Wales, 40 of the 60 seats are elected from the Westminster constituencies, with the remaining 20 being allocated on the basis of four from each of the five European constituencies. Using a similar version of AMS for the second chamber could be unpopular with members of the House of Commons. Altering the proportions in favour of having a greater number of topped-up seats might cast doubt on the Welsh and Scottish systems while not wholly removing the disadvantage of constituency seats.

Single Transferable Vote v. regional lists
The only two methods which involve no single-member seats are the List System and the Single Transferable Vote.

STV is generally accepted as producing the most proportionate results, although at the cost of considerable complexity and an outcome which can seem remote to voters who see their fifth choice getting elected. Its main supporters for the second chamber are the Liberal Democrats, who believe that STV should be introduced for both chambers.[12] Although they have recently supported the Jenkins proposals as a first step towards a more proportionate system, their formal policy still poses a potential long-term problem. Most others believe that the voting systems for the two chambers should be different to avoid rivalry. If the Liberal Democrats maintain the policy of wishing to introduce STV for the Commons too, this may be sufficient in itself to rule it out as a practical option for the second chamber.

A further problem, although not an insurmountable one, could be the size of the electoral units used under the single transferable vote. The system certainly requires multi-member constituencies, but these have not generally been seen to be as large as, for example, an English region. In order to meet the strong feeling that the second chamber should offer regional representation, STV would need to be organised on this basis. STV is used in an electorate of just over one million for Northern Ireland's election to the European Parliament. Furthermore, results are more proportionate the larger the constituency, so there is no reason, in principle, why it could not be organised to cover the largest region, the nearly five million voters of Greater London. The question of the most appropriate electoral system is obviously an area for the Royal Commission, affected perhaps, in this instance, by the view which the Liberal Democrat Party might take of its long-term policy.

The best system for the second chamber would be that of the regional list recommended by the Plant Committee and by Mitchell and Davies. It produces a second chamber with a regional voice. It avoids adopting an electoral system which could lead to tension with the Commons. It enables the second chamber to be representative of the widest possible range of opinion in an area. To function effectively, it should have wide legitimacy but at the same time the roles of revising and deliberating mean that its members should be at a greater distance than MPs from local needs and specific concerns. The task is not to represent individual constituents, fight for the needs of a specific constituency area or enable citizens to have access to the executive. It is to review what the primary chamber has done, looking both at the fine detail and at the bigger picture, freer of day-to-day concerns and pressures. To do this, the members will need access to information, arguments and expertise more than to the political feeling on the streets. A fair comparison is with the European Parliament.

As some MEPs told the Plant Committee, their main contact is with groups and organisations rather than with individuals.

Lists in operation

The Plant Committee suggested that the constituency boundaries should coincide with those of the future regional authorities as well as Scotland, Wales and Northern Ireland. Since it was published, of course, the Labour Government has implemented one of its two recommendations in this area by introducing regional lists for elections to the European Parliament. One of the advantages of using the same or similar systems for both sets of elections would be in not overburdening the electorate. Unlike using the same system as for the Commons, or AMS in Scotland, there would be no risk of unfavourable comparisons with the results of a constituency-based body.

Mitchell and Davies proposed that there should be an equal number of representatives from each nation and region (as is the case with senators representing states in the USA). We shall return to this issue in the final chapter.

On the European Parliamentary Elections Bill, as we have seen, criticisms were voiced concerning the role of political parties in ranking candidates. As the Plant Committee pointed out, the level of party patronage in constructing a list is lower than that involved in nominating members of the second chamber. There are, of course, versions of the list system which allow for voters to choose either to vote for the party ticket or to alter the position of candidates on the lists. Consideration should be given to opting for an open-list system for the second chamber. Political parties might also be encouraged to involve their members in the selection or ranking of candidates. Too much should not be made, however, of this issue. As Lord Williams of Mostyn pointed out in debating the European bill, parties would have the opportunity to promote on their lists female candidates and others such as those from ethnic minorities who might not otherwise achieve high rankings. In the same way, they could insert candidates for the second chamber whose skills, knowledge or regional experience fitted them well for the task of revising legislation, but whose political profile might not secure them a high place in an open selection process. This is an issue which the Royal Commission will be able to assess at first hand, since the European elections scheduled for June 1999 will take place while it is sitting.

The case for direct election

The natural democratic method
Direct election is the natural method of choosing legislators in a democracy. Many second chambers are directly elected, so there is obviously nothing inherent in their nature or in the process of revising legislation which makes it unsuitable for them. The onus is on those who do not support direct election to the second chamber to prove that another method is more suitable.

As we have already seen, the problems associated with nomination and indirect election are substantial. There are basic difficulties in principle: in the first case over who appoints; in the second, over voting for one body and invisibly affecting an election for another. Nor, in deciding the membership of the future second chamber of parliament, should we lose sight of the message it could send about our respect for democracy if we decide to choose its members by other means.

A legitimate second chamber
The main argument for reform, it will be recalled, is that the second chamber has been unable to do its job properly. Only a House with at least the majority of its members directly elected would have the legitimacy to make a bicameral legislature work. As the Canadian experience has demonstrated, a nominated House, although it would not be as supine as the Conservatives affect to believe, would still lack the basic legitimacy necessary to a legislative chamber. Likewise, a body incorporating indirect election would have insufficient standing. In one respect, it could be weaker since its members would be answerable to other bodies. The legitimacy which the members could claim would be not their own but that of

161

their nominating body, but, as we have seen, this would be compromised by their lack of accountability for many of the areas of scrutiny and revision. As part-timers whose primary focus was elsewhere, their position would be divided uncomfortably between the good opinion of those who appointed them and that of their party at Westminster. Approval at home, moreover, would be subject to factors very different from whether they were effective legislators.

After the disastrous experience of Conservative governments dominant for nearly two decades on a minority of the vote, in the face of which the second chamber was able to operate only imperfectly as a revising body, we should be on our guard against repeating by design the weakness handed down by history.

A stronger voice for nations and regions

It would not just be the second chamber which was more legitimate. The voice of the nations and regions of Britain would be stronger too. Nations and regions would be directly represented not just at their own and European levels, but also at Westminster; they would have a voice at three tiers, not merely at two. Rather than devolved and regional members dashing between their constituency, their assembly and London, the members of each tier would be free to concentrate on matters at their own level, cooperating with colleagues at the other two, but equally pursuing issues without divided loyalties where their interests did not coincide.

Direct election would substantially increase the weight behind the words and decisions of the representatives. The members in the second chamber would speak legitimately for voters in their nation or region across the whole range of matters in the UK parliament. Fundamentally, direct election would give a voice to the people of the nations and regions, rather than to their devolved institutions. It is they, rather than their devolved representatives, to whom their members in the second chamber would be accountable. This ties in closely with the Government's desire to boost what the Home Secretary has called 'people's sense of citizenship'.[13] The national and regional voice would be heard directly at the centre, rather than as an 'echo' through the national and regional bodies.

Nor would some of their representatives have an inferior status, as would occur if the second chamber contained both directly and indirectly elected members. The problem of English regional members representing bodies with fewer powers than their colleagues from Scotland, Northern Ireland and Wales would disappear; and with it a possible further strain on the devolution settlement.

The voice would be a political rather than an institutional one. Representatives' support would reflect the political views of the national/regional electorate across both Westminster and 'home' issues, such as employment, development and resources, which could significantly develop this country's excessively London-centred view of political issues.

Also, separating the second chamber from the devolved assemblies ought to avoid imposing any extraneous pressure on the Assembly in Northern Ireland, or raising issues as to the role and functions of its members, which might otherwise affect how the Good Friday Agreement is implemented.

Nor need this be disadvantageous to local government, for the reasons discussed earlier. It would avoid the complications of being drawn into national politics and of some of its leading members sitting on both sides of the table in discussions with government. As custodians of a new experiment, elected mayors could only benefit from having the time to do their job properly. The re-establishing of strong local government would be allowed to develop as an intrinsic good.

Bedding devolution down

As sometimes in local elections, the criticism may be heard that the electorate would vote along Westminster lines in elections for English regions – though perhaps not in those for the Scottish Parliament and Welsh Assembly. This would obviously not affect the credibility of directly elected regional members. The parties' respective support could, of course, differ between elections for the devolved/regional body and the second chamber levels, underlining the dangers of using indirect election as a barometer of opinion.

Direct election would avoid the problem of the devolved bodies and regional assemblies not having the same electoral cycles. A second chamber dependent on political trends and overlapping timetables could have a restless, shifting nature and a political balance subject to frequent change. While a directly elected body could be expected to have its own cycle, probably on a fixed term, which would operate independently from that of the Commons – perhaps even on a staggered basis – changes in its political balance would represent a gauge of opinion on matters affecting Westminster rather than be determined by changes in party support in other bodies.

Devolution and regionalism are important changes in the way we are governed which need to be taken seriously and given time to develop and bed down. Expecting too much of the members who will have to make them work, in terms of both their physical presence and the aspirations with which they are burdened, could be unhelpful. In Northern Ireland, it could have even more serious consequences. It would be better for members of the three new devolved bodies, and of the English regional assemblies when created, to be given the time and space to concentrate on their primary task, that of making devolution and regionalism a success.

Strengthening the Union

In terms of strengthening the Union, the 'constitutional glue' could be applied soon and without needing first to add more parts to the structure. The voice of the English regions could be heard without waiting for the creation of first regional chambers and then regional assemblies. This could be helpful in damping down emerging English objections to Scottish and Welsh devolution. It might also strengthen the cause of English regionalism by demonstrating its relevance to the whole country, smoothing the path for regional assemblies in Labour's second term.

Timing Lords and Commons reform together

Decoupling Lords reform from the creation of English regions could also remove a significant constraint on the timing of

Labour's constitutional reform programme. Lords reform could either proceed separately or be taken forward in parallel with the referendum on voting reform in the Commons – as Tony Blair and Paddy Ashdown have both hinted. The referendum question on electoral reform will be whether to retain first-past-the-post or to move to the Alternative Vote Top Up system of election. Both are constituency-based systems so the choice need not be affected by a proposal for a second chamber based on voting by regional lists.

An argument which should be tackled is that we cannot decide on a second chamber chosen by a form of proportional representation until the future voting system for the House of Commons is known. The case is that voting reform in the Commons might mean fewer strong single-party governments in the future and that the decision as to the desirable strength of the second chamber should follow from that choice. The argument is grounded in the British assumption of a strong executive: it sees the role of the second chamber (and the first) purely as functions of the relative strength of the executive, on which the structures of representation and the voting systems should depend. The reality should be the other way round.

The argument is also essentially unicameralist: if the first chamber is stronger, there is less need of a second. It ignores the value of different representation in the second chamber, acting as a counterweight to devolution. It overlooks, too, the possibility that in Britain, with its tradition of strong party loyalty, coalition governments could be just as likely to dominate the House of Commons as single-party administrations. Nor can it be assumed that a more proportional system is necessarily any guarantee against one-party dominance; the voting patterns of the future cannot be predicted.

The value of a second chamber, as we have argued, is in holding issues up to the light and asking for a second look. New functions for it, such as examining constitutional measures, could be equally important whatever the strength of the government of the day. The answer to this argument lies in the powers given to the second chamber and how they are used, rather than in its composition. The threefold objective of reform should be to ensure that: both Houses of Parliament have the legitimacy of a democratic and representative composition appropriate to their functions; as a result of their composition they are themselves in the correct balance; and, within that balance, the second chamber has adequate powers to perform its functions. The correct balance is clearly that the second chamber should be weaker than the Commons in its composition. In consequence, an executive with a majority there should be able ultimately to get its way. Once that balance has been achieved through composition, however, the way in which the powers are used becomes a matter for the political interplay between the executive, the Commons and the second chamber and new conventions which will inevitably develop to govern the process. There would doubtless be heavy political constraints applied to prevent a second chamber from overstepping the mark. In designing for the future, however, it is important that we do not shackle parliament with a second chamber which is too weak.

Getting the balance right

The instant conclusion, therefore, might be that option 5, the wholly directly elected House, is the answer. We shall deal with that in the next chapter. What is clear at this stage, however, is that direct election is the preferable principle, in general, on which to base a modern second chamber with the legitimacy to do its job. It also avoids the complications and possible contradictions for the new devolved and regional assemblies, which are inherent in the system of indirect election.

It would have, however, three significant disadvantages in the context of reform of the House of Lords:

- There could be a possibility of direct challenge to the superiority of the Commons.
- There would be no place for a politically independent element.
- One party might be able to command a majority.

The positions of the three main political parties are largely agreed on these points. On the third point, the Conservatives

166

have not made an explicit commitment to no single party having a majority but they support an independent element, which would be likely to produce that outcome.[14]

The first point is obviously the most serious. It is sufficient in itself to rule out a wholly elected House. In the absence of a written constitution, the supreme authority of the House of Commons needs to remain beyond doubt. Basing the voting system for the second chamber on units other than single-member constituencies would signal strongly that the Commons had the greater political legitimacy. This could obviously be made clear in creating the new body. While this might well be sufficient to sustain the position of the Commons, however, it might not be enough to prevent a challenge. The result could be disputes between the two Houses, especially where political control differed.

The third point links directly to the first. The possibility that one party – particularly a party not in power – could achieve a majority in the second chamber would be unlikely to prove acceptable to the Commons. There would be a substantial risk of a political stand-off, even in circumstances where the powers of the second chamber had been severely circumscribed. It would not merely be a mirror image of what we have at present.

In the case of retaining Crossbenchers, there is a widespread view that the involvement of non-political legislators in a political chamber has been a happy accident of the Westminster system. Many outside organisations have reason to be grateful to independent peers for the commitment and wisdom they have brought to bear on an issue, sometimes producing an unexpected success. As the activities of the Lords have become more widely known in recent years, there would be considerable opposition to the *de facto* removal of Crossbench members from the second chamber.

CHAPTER FIVE

A FULL REFORM PACKAGE

Three questions

Asking what sort of second chamber we want involves three questions:

- What should it be?
- What should it do?
- What should it represent?

These are interrelated. The first and last overlap as to who should be in it and what it stands for. The second – its role, functions and powers – is closely linked to its composition.

The answers to these three questions determine the shape of a coordinated package for reform of the Lords. Together with a look at the overall timetable for reform they form the subject of this chapter.

The position of the House of Commons

Before looking at this package, one issue has to be addressed immediately. It should be clear from what has already been said that the supremacy of the House of Commons must remain paramount in reforming the second chamber. The basis of the constitution as it has evolved from the 17th century is that the House of Commons is pre-eminent within a system of parliamentary sovereignty. The government of the

168

day derives its authority from the Commons, which has sole power over national taxation and spending and, under the Parliament Acts, the power ultimately to secure its legislation. Its pre-eminence rests on its status as the House which is wholly elected. That position has been underlined in recent discussions about its electoral system, enshrined in the Jenkins report, that the link between the MP and his or her constituency is an important facet of the system of representation. Whatever the result of the forthcoming referendum, preservation of the substance of the constituency link has been placed above strict proportionality as the goal of the electoral system for the House of Commons. Given the fears expressed in the past, notably in 1968/9, over the effect of Lords reform on the position of the Commons, its status as the 'primary' House must remain unchallenged. A package of reforms is possible which fully meets those concerns.

Indeed, the argument goes further. This country has not had a second chamber which has functioned properly for at least a century and probably much longer. In modern times, the second chamber has not had legitimacy. Parliament, as we have argued, has been virtually unicameral. The essential aim of reform should be to strengthen the second chamber to the point where it has the legitimacy *vis-à-vis* the government to perform its functions without threatening the position of the Commons. Government and Commons are often spoken of as though they were the same. For MPs of the governing party, of course, their interests are close, but they are not identical.

In a democratic age, any institution which has the power to ask an elected government to think again needs itself to be at least partly democratic. Nothing else will do in the end. If it is to be able to register its point, it needs some democratic legitimacy. Equally, if it is to exercise that power, it needs to be democratically accountable. The present House of Lords has been largely unable to ask governments to think again in a meaningful way because, since the coming of democracy, it has had no democratic right to do so. It would be folly to repeat the mistake by re-creating an undemocratic institution. If such a body sought to exercise its powers, it could well fail. If it exercised them wrongly, no one could hold it to account.

If it refused to exercise them, it would leave its functions unfulfilled.

The simple view that a functioning second chamber would weaken the primary chamber is too narrow. It assumes that there is a fixed amount of power between them, and that what one gains the other must lose. It is an approach which appears to favour governments (in the short-term). Administrations with their eyes on their own medium-term success or the judgement of history should be wary. For MPs, whichever side they are on, the argument is self-defeating. Provided the right balance is struck, a second chamber which illuminated new areas and revised legislation effectively without developing into a rival could greatly assist MPs, both in supporting government and in holding it to account. It could help the House of Commons to do its job. The result would not only be better government, but better for 'the Government' too. An administration would ultimately enjoy deeper national consent for its measures. Just as select committees in the Commons have improved the quality of government scrutiny, and the Committee on Delegated Powers in the Lords has obliged departments to think about the justification before expecting their ministers to defend taking wide powers, so a more effective second chamber would increase the prestige of parliament and buttress the position of MPs on both sides of the Commons as the primary legislators. It would also strengthen the position of ministers within their own departments. The ultimate benefit would be to increase pressure on officials to furnish ministers in both Houses with robust arguments and proposals. The level of political debate would be improved, producing policy which was more deeply scrutinised and better understood – and consequently more effective.

Having said that, there are clear criteria which reform should meet to secure the position of the House of Commons, so that it remains the only wholly elected chamber within parliament. Its democratic superiority would be reinforced by retaining an electoral system based on a strong constituency link with individual members. Even if the Jenkins recommendations were to be implemented, the

Commons constituency members would still be closer to the electors, both geographically and in terms of numbers, so that they would remain more representative than the second chamber. The House of Commons should retain the sole right to determine financial matters and its rights under the Parliament Acts. The period of delay for non-constitutional bills should be reduced, and the powers of the second chamber in relation to Statutory Instruments should be limited. The convention that the government of the day is made in the House of Commons should be reaffirmed, and to avoid confusion the function of the second chamber should be clearly defined.

We believe that an approach of this kind should reassure the Commons that their pre-eminent position in the constitution can be reaffirmed and safeguarded. Particularly will this be so if the period of delay which the House of Lords can impose on a bill is further reduced.

We now turn to the three main questions posed at the beginning of this chapter.

What should it represent?

It may be best to deal with the last of the three questions first. As the previous chapter made clear, there has been a growing consensus that the nations and regions of the country should be represented in the second chamber. The independent Constitution Unit, for example, has stressed the importance of establishing an identity for the second chamber. Most studies of Lords reform have concluded that it should contain representatives chosen at the level of regions and what are now the devolved nations.

Devolution in Scotland and Wales has transformed the constitutional terrain, offering enormous opportunities to those nations. Along with developments in Northern Ireland, it has relocated a very significant proportion of public policy-making outside Westminster. The development of English regions will apply the logic of devolution in a different way, adding further complexity to an already asymmetrical picture. As different parts of the country acquire a stronger sense of national or regional control and identity, so the value of a central expression of a United Kingdom identity becomes clearer. Representation in the second chamber offers a route to a shared identity which is political but which does not directly affect the control of the government of the country.

A reformed second chamber could be the missing piece of the constitutional jigsaw, serving as the pinnacle of the structure and a focus of unity. As we have seen, indirect election carries substantial problems of gaps in accountability, as well as practical difficulties and possible disadvantages for regional and possibly local government. A structure involving an element of direct election from the nations and regions, however, would achieve the same objective without the complications. It would give the people of each part of the country – rather than their institutions – a second direct voting stake in the Union, alongside their participation in elections to the House of Commons, and one bearing a specifically national or regional label.

As well as devolution and Lords reform itself, Labour's constitutional programme covers human rights, choice on voting reform, freedom of information and the revival of local government. The unifying theme is citizenship and the opportunities and responsibilities entailed in advancing democracy. Producing a more democratic and representative second chamber will be another step in developing the rights of the citizen and his or her opportunities to participate in the democratic process. At present, the citizen has access to government through the House of Commons. Reform could give the citizen access through the second chamber to the process of revising legislation and other types of scrutinising government as well.

What should it be?

The three methods of choosing members of the second chamber – nomination, indirect election and direct election –

have been examined. Each model for the composition of a reformed House is based on one of these or a combination. Houses based on nomination and indirect election suffer from considerable problems, both in principle and practice.

The interconnection between the core revising role, democratic legitimacy and democratic accountability is central. In a nominated House, both legitimacy and accountability are lacking. Indirect election can claim to produce greater legitimacy, although whether this would be sufficient in the face of an elected government is debatable. Accountability, however, would be too diffuse. The proliferation of bodies with differing electoral cycles nominating members would mean that – unlike an elected body facing an election – no single body of people could hold them to account on a single occasion if the powers were exercised wrongly.

As concluded earlier, direct election is, in principle, the best basis for bestowing legitimacy on a modern second chamber. We saw, too, that the best electoral system for the second chamber would be the regional list system as recommended by the Plant Committee for both the second chamber and the European Parliament (possibly with the opportunity, as Plant suggested, for voters to amend the order of a party's candidates).

However, if direct election is right in principle, we also saw that a UK second chamber which was wholly elected would suffer from three basic drawbacks. First, it could become a rival to the House of Commons. Second, there would be no place in it for non-political expertise. Third, one party could expect to enjoy an overall majority in it. If this were not the governing party, there would obviously be an increased risk of conflict with the Commons. For these three reasons, a wholly elected second chamber should be rejected.

A partly elected, partly nominated House

Given the objective – the most legitimate option consistent with the Commons' position and without the other basic drawbacks – the solution readily becomes apparent. A partly elected, partly nominated House, the fourth of the five options outlined, is the only one which meets all these requirements. Being only partly elected, it would lack the legitimacy to rival the Commons. Its nominated independent members would preserve the existing mix of politics and expertise in the House, which is unique to Westminster. The existence of the Crossbenchers would make it in arithmetical terms very difficult for the government or any other political party to wield overall control. (If the proportion of independent members in the House were sufficiently great, this would become effectively impossible.)

As an example, if there were a House of 300 in which 200 were elected (i.e., two-thirds elected), a party would need to win 151 out of the 200 democratic seats in order to have a majority of just one. For practical purposes, this would be impossible, especially with proportional elections under a list or similar system. In fact, one might argue that a political party which secured something like three-quarters of the popular vote actually deserved to control the second chamber! At the same time, it would preserve the benefits of direct election. First and foremost, it would give the second chamber enough legitimacy to do its job effectively. A part-elected chamber would then have sufficient standing to take a different view from the government of the day, but not enough to go too far. Its legitimacy would always be secondary to that of the Commons. The directly elected element would also meet the requirement that a second chamber with any teeth should be politically accountable for its actions. This seems to us to comply with the White Paper. For all of these reasons, we reject the argument set out in the White Paper (Chapter 8, paragraph 33) against a mixed House.

Representing the nations and regions
In the context of devolution, the nations and regions would acquire direct representation in parliament and a stronger say in the 'strong, small centre' of the UK. It would amplify the national and regional voices at the centre of the Union in comparison with indirect election by providing them with

representatives carrying their own democratic legitimacy. There would be no gaps in accountability or confusion over their proper scope to limit their standing in Westminster politics. English representation would not depend in the short-term on two layers of indirect election, and in the longer-term on the creation of regional assemblies. Direct regional representation in the second chamber could advance the cause of regionalism.

Regions would form very large constituencies, as they will for the European Parliament. A list system would allow a wide range of views to be represented (including independents, at least in theory) and this could create a more pluralist and inclusive body. It would be open to the political parties to ensure that women, those from ethnic minorities and disabled people were properly represented. Lists would enable them as well to put forward candidates who had different types of experience, perhaps from business, the community or professional practice in the nations and regions. Such people might be highly suitable to a chamber which was part legislative and part deliberative but who would be unlikely to stand for the Commons and have less interest in a post in government.

The second chamber could also be a natural forum for those with political interests who had chosen, perhaps at an earlier stage, not to make the substantial sacrifices in terms of career and other interests which seem too often to be necessary in order to compete for a Commons seat. It would be a natural route upwards, too, for members of the devolved bodies, regional assemblies and local government, who would achieve a greater standing in their own right than by indirect election. Others, such as former MPs with regional roots, could bring valuable parliamentary experience. It would also be an excellent development if parties were to promote younger candidates – perhaps from regional or local government – who might see a spell in the second chamber as a useful stepping-stone to a seat in the Commons. In the early years of the reformed chamber, it might assist continuity and the transition to the new structure if the parties were to encourage existing life peers – many of whom boast precisely the range of experience described – to seek election as regional representatives.

Independent members

The criticisms of nomination as a system matter far less if the House is not dependent on it for its membership and rationale. In any case, the argument that life peers can be expected to exercise independent judgement stands up more strongly for non-political than for political peers. The expertise and experience of appointed Crossbenchers and independents clearly 'add value' to a revising chamber and should only be discarded for a good reason. In a House most of whose members were elected, they would continue to have a substantial contribution to make. Even the possibility that, if they remained life peers, their average age might, over time, exceed that of the elected members need be no disadvantage.

An open process could be established, based on the Appointments Commission proposed in the White Paper, to secure representation on the Crossbenches across a range of occupations, skills and experience. These could cover the public, private, academic, voluntary and religious sectors, the starting point being the type of experience and representativeness sought as well as the distinction of the individual concerned. The Appointments Commission, translated into a permanent body, could establish consultative arrangements with the widest possible range of organisations.

The Crossbenchers would become more, not less, significant numerically in a reformed House with a mixed membership. At present, while their contributions to debate are often influential, their impact in the lobbies often has less effect. This is partly because their own levels of attendance vary, but also because of the regular preponderance of Conservatives. A reformed House will be more politically balanced, and the Crossbench vote could more often be pivotal. In a part-elected, part-nominated House it might be appropriate to apply an attendance requirement to non-party peers. New members could be recruited as working peers able and willing to attend regularly through a given number of sittings of the House, on the basis that the role of the Crossbencher should

176

be to exercise an independent judgement on the business as a whole as well as to contribute to debate in a specialist area.

Honours system

There need be no significant effect on the awarding of peerages under the Honours system. Most peerages would continue to be granted for distinguished service, but need no longer carry a seat in the second chamber. Suitable potential recipients could be approached via the Appointments Commission, acting in concert with those advising the Queen on honours, to inquire whether they would wish also to take on membership of the second chamber as part of their honour. In effect, therefore, peerages would be awarded for two purposes: as honours in themselves, and as the qualification for a non-elected person to sit in the second chamber, with no reason why the two should not coincide in a suitable case. New Crossbenchers might be asked to add a suffix (such as the suggested 'ML' or Member of the Lords) to their name to distinguish them as a parliamentary peer. The distinction could be made in legislation, or, if this were not acceptable, those not joining the work of the House could simply be asked to take leave of absence.

Bishops and members of other faiths

Bishops would remain under this model, and religious representation might well acquire a stronger role in a reformed chamber. As with the Crossman reforms, the Church of England might agree that the number of its bishops with ex-officio seats could be reduced. This need have no significant effect on its voice in the chamber, since bishops have too many other commitments to allow more than a minority of them to attend at any one time. It is comparatively rare for more than eight or nine of the 26 bishops and archbishops to vote at once. As an alternative to reducing the strength, a rota could limit the effective number. The purpose would be to create places for representatives of other faiths to join. This would, one hopes, reinvigorate the concept of a spiritual and moral dimension to the work of the House, expanding the unique role which the bishops have long played, and which many would agree should have a valuable place in a country's approach to its political and social problems. Maintaining a distinction between Anglican bishops who sat ex-officio and representatives of other faiths appointed as life peers on the advice of the Appointments Commission might assist in disentangling this question from that of the position of the established Church.

Law lords and the Lord Chancellor

The position of the law lords is, as the White Paper noted, anomalous in the context of any supposed separation of powers. It is possible, although perhaps not likely, that recent controversies over the hearing of the Pinochet case in the House of Lords might affect the process of appointment of law lords or, in the longer term, the exercise of the judicial role of the House. At present, their interventions in debate are generally considered helpful and well informed, and their involvement might be expected to continue unless the Royal Commission were to take a different view on the principle.

The position of the Lord Chancellor, however, who combines a judicial and an executive role, could obviously become more complicated in a partly elected House, unless the person appointed were already a member of that House. It might, however, be considered inappropriate for an elected person to act as head of the judiciary. A limited solution might be for the position of Lord Chancellor temporarily to remain a political appointee with a life peerage.

Wide support

Almost every scheme for reform of the House of Lords since the 1970s has incorporated the principle of direct election. The majority of those schemes in fact proposed a wholly elected House, mostly using different forms of proportional representation and generally varying in size between 300 and 500 members, with one reaching 625.[1] The remainder proposed part election and part nomination and opinion seems clearly to have moved in favour of this model in recent years. Policies have been advanced in, and by, each of the three main political parties for either a wholly or a partly elected House.

Labour's policy has supported both models at different times in the recent past. Its manifesto in 1992, for example, promised reforms leading to 'a new elected second chamber' which would have the power to delay for the lifetime of a parliament legislation reducing individual or constitutional rights. The Plant Committee in 1993 reflected the same policy in rejecting nominees in favour of a fully elected second chamber. The position changed before the last general election in the direction of retaining some independent nominees in an otherwise elected second chamber. Tony Blair, giving the John Smith Memorial Lecture in February 1996, said: 'We have always favoured an elected second chamber,' but went on to draw attention to Ivor Richard's proposal that distinguished nominated members might also remain.

The joint Labour/Liberal Democrat report of the Joint Consultative Committee on Constitutional Reform, published in March 1997 (and better known as the Cook/Maclennan report), was less specific. It said that there was a 'valuable continuing role' for a non-party element and that both parties believed that the Crossbenches should remain at about one-fifth of the House after the hereditary peers left. Prefiguring the 1997 Labour manifesto, it stated that a joint committee of both Houses should bring forward 'recommendations for a democratic and representative second chamber'.

The Liberal Democrat Party believes that the second chamber should remain an important 'check and balance' on the House of Commons.[2] There should be a 'predominantly directly elected element'. The optimum size should be considered by the joint committee proposed in the Cook/Maclennan report, but they propose some 300 members, of whom around 250 (i.e., five-sixths) should be elected. Members should be elected from Scotland, Wales, Northern Ireland and the English regions under the STV system for six-year terms with one-third facing re-election every two years.

The Home Committee
The last official Conservative examination of the issues, before the Mackay Commission established by William Hague, reported in 1978.[3] The committee, under the former

Prime Minister, Lord Home, produced a detailed blueprint for a House which it considered should have two 'major and interdependent roles': revising legislation and 'the provision of a measure of constitutional safeguard' which it considered the 'essence of the case' for a strong second chamber.

Not counting bishops and law lords, this House would have 402 members. Two-thirds would be elected by proportional representation for a nine-year term with elections every three years. If a regional list system were adopted for the European Assembly (now the European Parliament), 'it would seem sensible to use the same system in elections for the second chamber'. It also foresaw that if devolution developed, direct elections to the second chamber would offer a means to represent those regions and devolved nations at Westminster. One-third would be appointed members, chosen on the advice of a committee of the Privy Council. Appointed members, too, would serve for a nine-year term. Members would receive a salary and all members would be called Lords of Parliament (as in the Crossman proposals). Either the appointed members would all have been Crossbenchers, recruited from 'persons of distinction in public life', or they could have included political appointees from outside bodies such as future regional or local government, the devolved assemblies (which were then expected to be created under the Callaghan Government's plans for devolution), or members of the European Parliament. As the report pointed out, however, retaining Crossbenchers would lessen the likelihood of conflict with the Commons. It would also enable law lords and bishops to stay and representatives from other faiths to be included. The committee proposed that the bishops be reduced to 16 in number, with 12 law lords, producing a total membership of around 430.

The Home Committee considered proposing indirectly rather than directly elected members for the non-appointed element. The report said that it was doubtful that a second chamber composed in that way would have sufficient legitimacy. Indirect election had not been successful or popular in Britain. Resistance had been an important element in abolishing aldermanic seats in local government and the committee seemed unimpressed with its continued existence (as in the then Inner London Education Authority). It also considered that while a wholly nominated House replicating the party balance in the Commons might be an effective revising chamber, it would be unable to act as a constitutional safeguard.

The former Conservative Prime Minister, John Major, has declared his support for a mixed House.[4] The former Leader of the Lords, Lady Young, who was a member of the Home Committee, said in a debate on Lords reform that she stood by its proposals. Lord Baker of Dorking, the former Home Secretary and another of its members, praised it in the same debate and said that he supported a mixed composition.[5]

In 1998, Nicholas Kent of the Tory Reform Group published a detailed proposal for a mixed House which he described as rather in the manner of the Home report. Just over half of the voting members would be elected. In a House of 350 (of whom 300 were voting members), 160 would be elected regionally for a nine-year term either by a proportional system or by first-past-the-post. Most of the non-elected members would be life peers. Fifty hereditary peers would remain as non-voting members.

There is support, too, for a part-elected House from outside the political parties. Charter 88 believes that the second chamber should be 'primarily an elected body' in which no party has a majority and a wide range of interests is represented. The voting system should be as proportional as possible. It comes down, on balance, in favour of supporting 'the need for the second chamber to have access to expert advice'. It believes, however, that the chamber itself rather than the government should appoint the non-elected members.

Mitchell and Davies reported in 1993 in favour of a predominantly elected body to be called a Senate. The chamber should have 270 elected members and 30 appointed members. Both types would serve for fixed terms of nine years, a third being replaced every three years. The Senate would thus not be subject to dissolution. Election would be by the regional list system. They recommended that rather than allocate numbers of representatives by population, each region should return the same number. Appointments would be made by a joint committee of both Houses and approved by the Prime Minister. Appointees could serve for one term only. Membership of the body would be a salaried full-time job.[6]

The two-thirds elected, one-third nominated model

The proportions suggested for election and nomination range from a House which is 90 per cent elected (Mitchell and Davies, IPPR) to one which is just over half elected (Kent, TRG). We believe that the two-thirds elected model strikes the best balance, with the one-third who are nominated being non-political members appointed for their expertise and willingness to take a full part as independents in the work of the House.

Supporting a democratic proportion of two-thirds, rather than a greater figure, might seem to be unduly limiting the elected element. We do not take that view. A House composed in this way would be predominantly directly elected. It would have increased democratic legitimacy. At the same time, the nominated element would be substantial, involving the creation of a greater proportion of appointed independent members than are currently on the Crossbenches as life peers. This would be an advantage in terms of the acceptability of the new House. The higher the proportion of non-political members, the lower the likelihood of clashes with the Commons. Its legitimacy would clearly be secondary to that of the House of Commons as the only wholly elected chamber. The numbers on the Crossbenches, amounting to a 'blocking third', would, as we have seen, make it virtually impossible for one party to control the second chamber. In practice, the politics of the second chamber would tend away from extremes and focus attention on the political centre of gravity on the Crossbenches.

It has been argued that there would be strains between the two types of members, particularly if votes were carried against the government of the day with the support of the non-elected members. The opposite is more likely. Since the two types of members would have an entirely separate status, and a majority of the non-political members would often have to support a division against the government in order for it to be carried, this would be more likely to promote cross-working and mutual respect. The government of the day could attract criticism if it simply attacked distinguished independent members as unelected, since the House would deliberately have been set up on a mixed basis of merit and election. In fact, the blocking third of Crossbench votes could be pivotal. They could prevent game-playing by Opposition parties, but equally lend weight to a national issue on which there was consensus.

The present House of Lords, of course, has a mixed political/independent membership, which is one of its unique feature. If the Alternative Vote Top Up system is introduced in the House of Commons, it too will have more than one type of member. Scotland and Wales will also shortly have two types of members, with additional members elected under a proportional allocation of seats. We are moving to a more mature view of plural politics. Ultimately, however, the relationship between the two Houses would be founded on the Commons' right to get its way.

Size and cycles
Another important factor in the relationship with the Commons will be the size of the second chamber. It will be important that the second chamber is smaller than the primary one. As a result, MPs should be clearly seen to be closer to their electorates, by virtue not merely of the constituency structure but in terms of the average number each respectively represents. In its recommendations for the electoral system for the second chamber, the Plant Committee took a quota under the list system of 135,000 voters or twice the number of an MP's total electorate. We would suggest that the quota might be slightly higher, but it will be clear that with such differences of scale there can be no argument as to which type of representative has the closer link with their electorate.

The Home Committee proposed a House of 430 members. At that level, the second chamber would still be larger than in other countries and the Royal Commission will no doubt wish to be satisfied that there was a role for that number of members. A factor to be borne in mind is obviously the starting point of the interim House which will number some 500 life peers, plus the 91 hereditary peers. Most of these peers would no doubt expect to continue to play a role and it would probably prove unpopular to aim for a much smaller House, at least at the outset. One possibility might be to move over time to a smaller House, if this were desired. The Royal Commission will undoubtedly wish to take a view on the desirable size of whatever model it recommends. A list system would make it relatively easy over a period of time to alter the number of elected members.

In defence of the sort of size proposed by Home, it is worth pointing out that in this country we are used to very large numbers of parliamentarians by comparison with the numbers elsewhere. As we have seen, the average daily attendance now exceeds 400. Significantly reducing the size of the second chamber might be expected to raise questions as to whether the size of the House of Commons ought also to be reviewed. A smaller number of Crossbench places would obviously limit the range of appointments which could be made. It is also implicit in the role of Crossbenchers, even if not of elected members, that they have other commitments and interests and that, even though there was an expectation that they would attend through a third or more of sittings, this would still mean that only very rarely would all be present at the same time.

Our proposal is that – at least at the outset – the membership should be in the range 400–450, but that the upper figure should be seen very much as the maximum. The Royal Commission might like to consider whether a smaller size would allow sufficiently broad representation across the nations and regions, as well as among independents. If it were feasible, over time, figures of 366 (244 of whom would be elected) or even 300 (200 of whom would be elected) might be considered. A figure of 450 would represent 300 elected and 150 appointed members.

The Plant Committee recommended a wholly elected House of 322 members. Its analysis was based on the nine standard regions in England together with Scotland, Wales and Northern Ireland. The number of members ranged from eight in Northern Ireland to 59 in the populous South-East, with an additional 36 members from London. Scotland would send 29 members, with 10 from Wales.

If the House were to number 450, the Plant figures could be applied to the elected element with a smaller reduction in the number of representatives from each region (or, technically, an increase in the quota for election under the list) to produce an elected element of about 300 members.

If elections to the second chamber took place at the same time as those to the House of Commons, there would be a danger that the position of a newly elected government could be weakened. A fixed term avoids this danger and represents a further important distinction between the Commons and the second chamber. An electoral cycle of nine years, with elections every three years, would be sufficiently long to emphasise the more detached nature of representation in the second chamber. Furthermore, staggering elections would dampen the effect of swings in public opinion on its political balance, underlining stability in its role and limiting the degree to which it could be politically antagonistic to the Commons.

Different models propose an equal number of places for each region, a weighting of places either in favour of less populous areas or in recognition of the special positions of Scotland, Wales and Northern Ireland, or (as Plant and Home proposed) an equal basis of representation by population. Although a limited degree of weighting might be an issue for the Royal Commission to assess, we consider that equality according to population should be emphasised. This would provide the greatest opportunity for diversity and the representation of a wide range of views. It would also avoid the possible danger of appearing to disadvantage some or all of the English regions at an important point in their development.

On appointed members, the Home report proposed that they should be appointed for a term of the same duration as the elected members to underline the cohesiveness of the House. While acknowledging the point, the balance of advantage – especially in a House elected in thirds – is with the continuation of life peerages separated from the Honours system as we have described. This would allow the maximum independence to the non-political members, and underline an element of continuity with the present House.

At present the two Houses have differing rules for disqualification from membership. The second chamber should adopt those of the Commons: sentence to prison for more than a year; detention in a mental hospital; expulsion by resolution of the House.

What should it do?

Of course, what really matters is the part a reformed second chamber can play in a parliamentary democracy. The five existing functions of the House are:

1. revising legislation
2. acting as a constitutional check and balance
3. scrutinising the executive
4. investigating issues not covered by the Commons
5. providing a forum for debate where the fate of the government is not normally in question

Each of these activities is valuable. There would seem to be no good reason to end any of them. They should remain and be developed by differing degrees. The final two have a clear place in the second chamber, as the White Paper indicates. The first three deserve more detailed examination and some new functions can also be suggested.

Revising legislation: the issue of powers

The present powers of the Lords mean that it can:

- delay all non-money bills for at least one year
- send amendments to bills back to the House of Commons
- vote down statutory instruments

The European Parliamentary Elections Bill showed that the Lords may send back amendments repeatedly provided one or other of the Houses changes the wording to avoid a deadlock, but that, although confronting the Commons six times was possible under the rules, it was unprecedented and has been seen as a breach of convention.

Bearing in mind the need for a structure of powers which allows the second chamber to be effective in its revising role while respecting the superiority of the Commons, and taking as a starting point the checklist of possible changes in the White Paper, a package of new powers appropriate to a partly-elected chamber would be as follows:

- Reduce the normal delaying power on legislation, perhaps to a fixed six months if the Commons have re-approved the measure in the intervening period. (The Home Committee believed, in contrast, that the power should be increased by restoring the pre-1949 power to delay bills for two years, perhaps only for the three years after an election – i.e., to slow down a government if it lost popularity near to the end of its term). We do not agree with this proposal.
- Keep the present delaying power (or one fixed at twelve months) for constitutional or human rights measures (see below). As with the general power, a delaying power fixed for a period rather than over a session would be more easily understood.
- Apply the Parliament Acts to all public bills, whichever chamber they start in.
- Define rejection of a bill as including returning the same issue (as defined by the Speaker of the House of Commons) three times to that House, whether or not on the same amendment.
- As proposed by Home, create a joint conciliation committee of both Houses which would intervene after both Houses had voted twice on an issue. The committee would have the right to propose compromise wording, recommend a cooling-off period or ask the government to report further. It would be chaired by a member of either House nominated by their respective Speaker. Interestingly, a conciliation process existed in the early nineteenth century, at

187

a time when a bill would fail if there was even one stage of disagreement.[7]

- Replace the present Lords' power to veto statutory instruments with either a short delaying power (e.g., one month) or a power to give the government the opportunity to re-present the same instrument if rejected in the second chamber, in order that the Commons could pass it and override the Lords.

We are not in favour of restoring to the second chamber the financial powers it lost in 1911.

One further issue would be whether any new conventions to modify or substitute for these rules should be negotiated between the political parties. If the powers over statutory instruments were regularised, there would be no further need for the current weak convention in that area. Other conventions governing more minor areas of practice would doubtless evolve as the two Houses interacted over time. Nevertheless, the question really concerns the Salisbury Doctrine. The original circumstances surrounding the doctrine were of a Conservative-dominated House facing a Labour Government with an overwhelming majority. The Doctrine has moved on, however, in two ways: first, it applies in the present House to second readings of all manifesto bills, whatever their political colour, and arguably to all second readings of government bills (with notable exceptions such as the War Crimes Bill, on which there was a free vote in both Houses); second, it appears to apply to wrecking amendments as well as to outright rejection (although apparently not, in the minds of the present Opposition, to delaying a bill beyond the end of the session). Would the doctrine logically fall away from a reformed House? The 'parties' to the agreement would have changed. Under the new regime, the House would probably have weaker powers than those it formerly enjoyed when the doctrine was formulated. Given the recent doubt as to the extent of the doctrine, it would make good political sense not to rely on convention to define the fundamental relations of the two Houses. It could, moreover, be thought either wrong in principle or simply impractical to limit the activities of a

House with some democratic legitimacy by means of convention. The better outcome would be to define a formal balance in the powers of the two Houses, such as suggested above, so that no convention is necessary.

Revising legislation: updating legislative scrutiny

There are a number of ways in which these powers could be put to better use in a reformed House. A Hansard Society Commission on the legislative process in 1992 recommended, for example, that both Houses should make better use of inquiries and evidence from outside experts in scrutinising legislation.[8] It also proposed that the operation of every major act and the delegated legislation made under it should be reviewed some two to three years after its enactment.[9] The Commons have already looked at a number of these proposals as part of the programme being carried out by the Select Committee on Modernisation but they could also be taken up by the second chamber.

Taking evidence before debate on a bill commences

Pre-second reading scrutiny could work as follows.[10] A published bill, together with memoranda from the department explaining its provisions, would be sent to a select committee. The relevant minister would be invited to give evidence on the policy, assisted by civil servants on factual and technical questions. The purpose would be not to debate the bill but to elucidate its meaning. Outside organisations could be invited to submit written evidence; conflicts of fact or interpretation could be pursued in oral evidence. A report would be produced prior to second reading.

The government would need to present its facts and arguments more fully than is now necessary for oral debates, but these demands are commonplace in departmental select committee and should hold no fears where policies are soundly based. Ministers would have the advantage, currently denied them, to test the water and make adjustments before cementing their position at second reading. Nor, in terms of timing, need the process lose the government much time. The sessions might last no longer than two weeks for a major bill and provision for this could be made under standing orders. Allowing for notice to witnesses might mean a total of four weeks between publication of the bill (or its reception from the Commons) and its second reading; or about two weeks longer than at present. The time saved at both the second reading and in later debates through clarifying the issues, answering factual points and identifying the core disagreements could easily make up this deficit. In practice, to make such a system work would require no more of government in terms of business management than that it publish its Lords bills two weeks earlier but costing it no time overall.

Looking at the ministerial powers

As already mentioned, the Delegated Powers and De-regulation Committee was created in 1992, partly in response to wide concern over ministers taking so-called 'Henry VIII' powers, which allow them to use secondary legislation to amend Acts of Parliament. The Committee examines bills to see whether such powers lurk in the drafting and should be drawn to the attention of the House, and deliberates on whether powers in a bill will be subjected to the appropriate level of scrutiny.

Scrutinising bills for the powers conferred on the executive is a natural role for a second chamber and links directly into its primary task of revising legislation. The Committee is widely recognised to have been a success and its approach has already affected the way in which government officials approach the drafting of legislation. It would be helpful if it looked at Commons bills before they came to the second chamber. In a reformed House, particularly if legislative scrutiny were to be improved, the role of screening out inappropriate government powers in advance should be better understood. Since the Commons do not scrutinise in this way, the second chamber could be given the function of doing so on behalf of parliament as a whole.

Improving the committee stage

In recent years, and particularly since the Labour Government came into office, the House has more frequently taken committee stage off the floor. There are various models but the most often used is Grand Committee, a more intimate committee-type examination of bills which all peers may, nonetheless, attend.

Amendments are moved and debated, although, by agreement, divisions are avoided. Speeches are less formal. The full transcript is published in the daily Hansard in the same way as proceedings in the chamber. The process tends to be used for less controversial bills or where the issues are complex and the government recognises that questions may remain to be resolved. In the Labour Government's first session, examples were the National Lottery Bill and the Data Protection Bill. Under the last Government, the Charities Bill was a measure taken successfully through a similar procedure for committee off the floor, with a number of worthwhile amendments being made. A reformed second chamber might be expected to expand its work in committees in a number of ways. In a mixed chamber where the government has less need to be the dominant player it might be appropriate to adopt models of this kind rather than the more formal standing committees of the Commons. This would preserve the beneficial features of committees of the whole House, which play an important part in the revising and scrutiny functions of the second chamber.

Scrutinising the implementation

Much of an Act of Parliament is implemented through delegated legislation. In view of the burden which this places on parliament (and which it addresses inadequately), the mechanics of scrutiny could usefully be streamlined.

At the moment the two Houses, through a joint committee, scrutinise whether instruments fall within the powers delegated to ministers. It would be possible, once they had been cleared as to 'vires', for instruments subject to the negative procedure (which at present receive little attention) to be graded as to importance. This explicit interest in their content would go beyond how most instruments are scrutinised at present. Most could be passed at that stage as entirely straightforward, but among the remainder the second chamber could then take the lead, inviting written evidence from departments and key outside groups and producing a report within the 40-day praying period. Instruments of medium-level importance would, in practice, be screened only in the second chamber, probably in a committee. Those of high-level importance, or those where the scrutiny committee had expressed concern, could be debated and voted upon in the second chamber and then be passed to the Commons. In practice, as now, the Commons would debate only major instruments, but, unlike now, MPs would have far more information since this would take place with the benefit of a full report and an earlier debate. Under the revised powers suggested above, the Commons would take the final decision on any instrument.

Although a fast-track procedure might be needed for very urgent cases, professional representative bodies would almost certainly be prepared to provide comments quickly if they were routinely involved in detailed scrutiny in this way.

Asking later how well the Act worked
Monitoring the effectiveness of legislation in its first two to three years would, over time, give parliament more reliable yardsticks with which to assess whether current proposals were likely to achieve their objectives. The Hansard Society saw this as a role for departmental select committees in the House of Commons. Many Acts of Parliament, however, cross departmental boundaries and the political issues involved will frequently make the process uncomfortable for MPs. In fact, a mixed second chamber, which had political credibility but no government majority and in which independent experts continued to play a role, could make a significant contribution in this area. The process would be similar to that employed in select committees in both Houses, with interested organisations invited to submit evidence within the scope of the inquiry and witnesses, including ministers and officials, called to examine areas deserving further exploration.

A stronger constitutional check and balance

The present House has a formal constitutional role over extensions to the life of a parliament or the removal of a judge, but while theoretically important these are limited in practice.

On the other hand, in exercising their legislative function in recent years, the Lords have been seen to be standing up for constitutional rights. This role could be developed so that a reformed House took on a special duty in relation to constitutional or human rights matters. The Labour Party manifesto for the 1992 general election made proposals along these lines. Such a role could take the form of monitoring and reporting on constitutional developments, such as devolution, as they bed down in future years.

How would this work? There could be a new delaying power to give it teeth in dealing with legislation. A list of relevant constitutional legislation could be drawn up which could only be amended under this procedure, together with a mechanism by which subsequent provisions could be added and draft bills certified as to whether they fell within the process (perhaps by the Speaker of the Commons). Existing enactments on the list would include the devolution legislation, Human Rights Act, European Communities Act together with any future freedom of information legislation, and older statutes such as the Bill of Rights and Act of Settlement. Since the constitutional position of the monarchy rests partly on these statutes, the second chamber could acquire the *de facto* role of protecting it.

Constitutional lawyers have long disputed whether it is possible to entrench major legislation, given that the doctrine of parliamentary sovereignty requires that a parliament should not have the power to bind its successors. Introducing a special power of delay for the second chamber would not amount to entrenchment, not could the views of the second chamber be predicted, but it does offer a way of marking the importance of certain types of legislation and allowing a longer period for objections and second thoughts. Others' suggestions might be to allow the second chamber to block a measure until the next election, to call for a referendum, or to allow the government to override a twelve-month delay if a referendum approved the measure in the meantime.

Where only part of a bill involved a constitutional matter, the longer delaying power would apply only to those provisions; in practice, if it were delayed it would probably have to be divided into two bills so that the non-constitutional parts could proceed.

A separate process involving the second chamber might be devised to oversee those parts of the constitution which rest on convention and the common law rather than statute. A special select committee of the House could be convened from time to time, for example, to advise it on constitutional questions arising from both legislation and elsewhere. Where the matter came from convention or common law, the House could pass a resolution for guidance.

In relation to human rights, the independent Constitution Unit proposed in 1996 that the second chamber could report on the UK's compliance with the European Convention and other international obligations.[11] The Human Rights Act 1998 has since incorporated the Convention into domestic law. The second chamber could report on its early years of operation. This could include monitoring the number of cases brought to the UK courts and the use of the fast-track procedure under the Act for amendments to the law. It could report on the effectiveness of procedures for compliance and identify any further gaps in the law or in public policy. While the courts have the role under the Act of giving effect to the legislation, the second chamber could monitor progress and promote awareness of human rights and their legal protection. This task might be particularly appropriate if the reformed chamber continued to contain law lords, who would be directly involved.

Better scrutiny of the executive

The government is scrutinised every day in the second chamber as in the first and this should doubtless continue after reform and develop in response to need. Any diminution in scrutiny would have to be heavily justified in an age where the power of party in the Commons has been joined with that of mass communications outside to strengthen the executive as never before.

It has been suggested that ministers should not continue to sit in the second chamber. It can be argued that the House would be more independent if members of the governing party did not feel the need to support their own members sitting on the frontbench, and that a wider range of scrutiny would be possible if ministers in general could be summoned to answer questions or to speak in debates. It is true that Lords ministers speak for the whole of their departments and often do not have direct responsibility for the precise issue under discussion. In theory, if the government does not depend on a majority in the second chamber, it may have no need of ministers there.

The White Paper makes it clear that the Government does not support this idea. Nor do we. Calling in ministers for whom the House and its members will be relatively unfamiliar erects a distance between scrutineer and scrutinised which would tend to formality and rigid exchange. A comparison might be made with relations between members of the US government and Congress, or the process of questioning EU Commissioners in the European Parliament. For more than two hundred years the Westminster model has been characterised by the presence in parliament of the members of the government. To move away from that system towards a more formal separation of powers in one chamber but not the other would be anomalous and could start to affect the way in which the House of Commons is organised. It is important to appreciate that although the system whereby the government is placed in the Commons is regulated by statute (to limit patronage), it is in itself a matter of convention and therefore in principle open to change without a formal decision. It is unlikely that removing ministers with direct accountability to, and knowledge of, the House and its members would strengthen its primary function of revising legislation. The short-term result would probably be simply to reduce the accountability of government in general as it became more remote.

The Lords' scrutiny of European policy and legislation is widely praised in the EU, where it is sometimes considered to be the best available. This is an obvious area for a second chamber to pursue, offering again the opportunity to undertake a burden which the Commons fails to shoulder fully and to carry it out in ways which assist both Houses. The role could comprise, for example, more in-depth investigations into specific issues as well as wider general scrutiny of European developments with the aim of 'demystifying' them.

Timetable for reform

Moving ahead on a part-elected, part-nominated model would enable reform of the second chamber and electoral reform for the Commons to be considered either in tandem at a referendum or separately, as seems most appropriate in the Government's overall timing.

If the Cranborne deal holds, the timetable from now on should see stage one enacted by autumn 1999. Most hereditary peers would leave before the next Queen's Speech. The Royal Commission should be able to report in time for legislation in the session 2000/2001 or 2001/2 in the run-up to the next general election (even if the Government thinks a brief joint committee is necessary to tidy up the details). If the election is called earlier than 2002, consensual proposals could appear in the manifestos of each of the parties. The last hereditary peers would leave on the introduction of the new second chamber. There would need to be transitional arrangements and possibly a phasing in, but the total life of the interim House before moving to further reform need be no more than two or three years.

CONCLUSIONS AND SUMMARY

THE OBVIOUS CONCLUSION of our examination of the possibilities for reform of the second chamber is that it is one of those issues which at first sight appears simple but in reality is one of enormous complexity. Yet none of the complications is insuperable provided the aim is kept firmly in mind.

The House of Lords is, or should be, the next most important democratic institution in our system of government after the House of Commons. Most observers now agree that the major constitutional need is for better scrutiny of the executive. Ultimately, it is in the executive's own interests to agree, though the parties always seem reluctant to recognise this when in government.

The fundamental aim in reforming the UK constitution is the planned reduction of centralised executive power. Indeed, it is central to the rest of Labour's programme of reform. Executive control over the House of Commons is stronger in Britain than in any comparable country. Though it frequently masquerades as a defence of the rights of the Commons, in reality many of the arguments against comprehensive reform are a defence of that executive power. Of course, Lords reform will make the second chamber more troublesome. That is both inevitable and, provided that the reformed second chamber has proper legitimacy and credibility, it is also right. Otherwise, we may as well have a unicameral legislature.

There are a number of issues which we are conscious are

left unanswered. The practicality of the transition to stage two is an example. There would be complex issues involved in a transition which we have not gone into in detail in a book of this kind. Our purpose is to assess the options and argue for a principle. Whatever option is adopted, other than the status quo after stage one, will involve practical questions which may mean that full reform has to be phased in over a period of time and in response to the sensitivities of individuals affected. There may, for instance, be a need for an attendance requirement for life peers applied to past years or to the future. Voluntary retirement might have attractions for some peers, not confined to those of retirement age. If a compulsory retirement age were introduced, it might be fairer to apply it to newcomers only. These would patently be matters for the Royal Commission and – probably more so – for the Joint Committee once a recommendation in principle had been accepted.

The basic approach in moving to the part-elected, part-nominated model is that the elected element, chosen by the regional list system, could be phased in over a period, perhaps using a nine-year term and staggered elections every three years.

The principle of parity of life peers in the White Paper, between the two main parties, given effect for the transitional House by Cranborne/Weatherill agreement, should be continued into the period in which a new House is phased in (what we might call the second transitional period). This would be necessary to enable the result of elections to be reflected in the political balance.

One other question mark is inevitably the as yet unknown approach of the Royal Commission. Its mandate is quite enough for it to be able to avoid the perils of overcaution. This is not a time for souls to be too timorous. If reform succeeds, there is a real opportunity – the first for nearly a century – to produce a sensible constitutional settlement between the two Houses of the British legislature and for it to last. But it does require vision and determination on the part of those most closely involved – the Royal Commission, the government and parliament itself. The Joint Committee of both Houses, presaged in the manifesto and the White Paper, will have to be a severely functional body. It is not the place to fight the arguments between the two Houses, and MPs on it will have a special responsibility to produce, or at least not to frustrate, an outcome which strengthens parliament as a whole.

In our view, neither nomination nor indirect election meets the basic need for a legitimate second chamber and overseas comparisons need to be qualified by the fact that in Britain the executive dominates the House of Commons to a greater extent than in any comparable country. Both systems also have basic problems of principle and practice, including, with indirect election, significant gaps in accountability. Nor might either be in the long-term interests of the nominating organisations and other political bodies. The Government has not named a preference. The July statements of the Prime Minister (and those in Opposition) appear to have been submerged.

Some might argue that both the approach in the White Paper (e.g., mixing up direct and indirect election) and specific statements in it amount to a steer to the Royal Commission towards a weak option – a nominated House with some indirectly elected members added. The latter might not even be elected people; nor might all of those involved in choosing them be. In practice, the line between nomination and indirect election is very blurred. There is, on the face of it, precious little to choose between them.

The real argument is not perhaps so much whether patronage of the living or the dead is preferable, but whether massive patronage of any kind is a suitable basis for membership of a second chamber.

Direct election is, after all, the only method by which true legitimacy is conferred and all sections of the population truly represented. There are great dangers in swapping one form of élite government for another.

Three 'qualifications', however, should be borne in mind:

- House of Commons supremacy must be maintained.
- No party should have an overall majority in the reformed House.

- we must preserve some independent members whose expertise and continuity will enable parliament as a whole to be better informed.

We believe that neither a wholly elected nor a wholly nominated model is satisfactory. A partly elected, partly nominated model, however, directly meets all the three qualifications.

The constitution should see a better balance between our desire for strong government within parliament and the rights of parliament itself; a degree of pluralism which brings other voices to bear but does not disrupt the basic system. To achieve this balance within a political system requires credibility and legitimacy, which in our view can only come from a predominantly (but not wholly) directly elected House.

The prize of a fully functioning parliament in which both chambers can operate more effectively is the objective. Reform should improve scrutiny and accountability and strengthen the role of parliament as a whole. We need change which empowers both Houses. Such a reform should not be misrepresented as mounting a challenge to the (largely theoretical) power of MPs.

The real choice faced by those who wish to reform the Lords is, in reality, whether we come down on the side of better governance or on the side of maintaining the relative ease which the present system gives to the executive. In our view, indirect elections would not fulfil that need. For the reasons outlined, we believe that a mixed House, with two-thirds of its members being directly elected and one-third being nominated, does.

Summary

1. The House of Lord is, or should be, the next most important democratic institution after the House of Commons. In the 1980s and 1990s, it was the Lords which provided some measure of balance to ideological government.
2. Lords reform is the most important item in Labour's con-

stitutional programme, apart possibly from devolution to Scotland.

3. Critics claim either that there will be no 'stage two' or that it will resemble stage one with perhaps some indirectly elected members added. While the Government has declined to state its preferred option, the White Paper includes pointers to the Royal Commission in the latter direction (chapter 8, paragraphs 23 and 35). A statement by the Prime Minister in July 1998 that stage two would be a 'more democratically elected Second Chamber' seems to have been submerged.

4. The Cranborne/Weatherill agreement to keep 91 hereditary peers until further reform links stages one and two. To fulfil its manifesto commitment, Labour will have to move to stage two before the next general election. Otherwise, the Conservatives could outflank them with their own proposals.

5. The timing of reform is unclear. While the Royal Commission is to report by 31 December 1999, and the White Paper says (although not consistently) that this is to enable the Government to make every effort to enact stage two by the next election, Ministers have also told the press that this is unlikely.

6. There are three reasons for reform: (i) the rationale for an aristocratic House has long disappeared; (ii) the present House is politically unbalanced; (iii) most important, its lack of legitimacy means that it cannot do its job as it should. Examples under the last government such as the poll tax (where it failed to relate the charge to ability to pay) are given in Chapter Two. Where it did manage to exercise its revising role (and the examples show the need) this was in spite of its composition.

7. The House of Lords performs five functions: (i) acting as a constitutional check and balance (omitted by the White Paper); (ii) scrutinising and revising legislation; (iii) scrutinising the actions of the executive; (iv) investigating issues which may not interest the Commons, or are too sensitive for it; (v) debating issues of national importance where the fate of the government does not hang in the

balance. It is also the final court of appeal.

8. The objective of reform should be to strengthen the second chamber to the point where it has the legitimacy *vis-à-vis* the government to perform its functions without threatening the position of the Commons. This requires that (i) both Houses have the legitimacy of a democratic and representative composition appropriate to their functions; (ii) as a result of their composition, they are themselves in the correct balance; (iii) within that balance, the second chamber has adequate powers to perform its functions.

9. The various models of membership (we exemplify five) are all variants of three basic methods: nomination; indirect election; and direct election. Each has advantages and disadvantages (see Chapter Four). The White Paper confuses direct and indirect election, making the latter appear more democratic.

10. A nominated House would have continuity and a range of expert opinion. Its basis would remain patronage, however, and only its non-party members would be independent. Life peers were introduced by the Conservatives to stave off more radical reform. A nominated House could amount to swapping rule by one élite for that of another and risks creating members who were delegates. It would be the weakest option and Canadian experience suggests it would be largely ineffective.

11. Indirect election could be seen as 'binding in' the nations and regions of the UK under devolution and giving them a voice at the centre. This has attractions but might not be the best way to do it. Putting, for example, Scottish MSPs into the second chamber could reopen arguments over devolution by giving them one set of responsibilities at Westminster and another at home. It could also hand a weapon to those seeking independence. Nor might indirect representation benefit regional or (if involved) local government. Members would be doing two jobs.

12. Indirectly elected members are accountable not to the electorate but to the body which nominates them. Since these would have narrower responsibilities than the

second chamber, there would be large gaps in members' accountability. A House of indirectly elected members would be unlikely, given the power of the UK executive, to have the legitimacy to fulfil its functions – as overseas examples suggest. The exception in the White Paper, the German Bundesrat, is a forum for negotiations between governments in a federal system.

13. Direct election is the natural method of choosing members in a democracy. Only a House with at least the majority of its members directly elected would have the legitimacy to make a bicameral system work in the UK. Equally, if it is to have the power to ask an elected government to think again, it should be democratically accountable. It would give the people of the nations and regions a stronger voice, while avoiding problems such as gaps in accountability and unbalancing devolution. The constitutional 'glue' could be applied without waiting for the creation of English regions.

14. A wholly elected House would suffer, however, from three significant drawbacks: (i) the superiority of the Commons could be challenged; (ii) there would be no place for an independent element; (iii) one party could command a majority.

15. A partly elected, partly nominated House meets all these objections for the very reasons that a wholly elected House does not: (i) its composition would be less legitimate than the Commons; (ii) it would retain the benefit of independent Crossbenchers; (iii) arithmetically (and especially if one third were Crossbenchers) it would be almost impossible for one party to control, underlined further by a proportional voting system. It would have sufficient legitimacy to perform its functions, but not too much. It would give a strong voice in a plural forum to the electorates of the nations and regions, while avoiding the disadvantages of indirect election. The White Paper's claim that this model could share many of the disadvantages of a wholly elected chamber is wide of the mark.

16. The ideal proportion would be two-thirds elected and one-third nominated (the latter all being independents),

following the recommendations of the Conservative Home Committee in 1978. This is close to Liberal Democrat policy and to where the Labour Party stood in the recent past.

17. In an ICM poll published in the *Guardian* (December 1998), 44 per cent thought the second chamber should be directly elected, 36 per cent supported one which was mainly directly elected but with a minority of appointed life peers, and 9 per cent said it should be made up of life peers only.

18. The powers of the second chamber should be regularised. The normal delaying power should be reduced to six months except for constitutional and human rights measures. All public bills should be brought within the Parliament Acts. The Commons should continue to determine financial matters. The power to send a bill back should be limited to three occasions and a conciliation committee should deal with disputes. The power to veto statutory instruments should be replaced by either a short delaying power or a Commons override.

19. The functions of the second chamber should be clearly defined. The five existing ones (point 7 above) should continue. Revision of legislation should be updated (e.g., taking evidence on a bill before debating it and monitoring its implementation). The second chamber could take on a special role in relation to constitutional or human rights matters and scrutiny of European policy and legislation could be strengthened.

20. The second chamber could be the missing piece of the constitutional jigsaw, promoting citizenship by directly representing the people of the nations and regions of the UK – rather than their institutions. This would give them a further direct voting stake in the Union, with a recognised national or regional label through a list system as recommended by the Plant Committee.

21. The executive's control over the House of Commons is stronger than in any comparable country. As the rest of Labour's constitutional programme has shown, the fundamental aim of reform is the planned reduction of cen-

tralised executive power. Though they often masquerade as a defence of the rights of the Commons, in reality many of the arguments against comprehensive reform are a defence of that power. Lords reform will, of course, make the second chamber more troublesome. It is both inevitable and, provided the second chamber has legitimacy and credibility, right. Otherwise, we might as well have a unicameral system.

22. A better balance between second chamber and executive, however, is not to be confused with challenging the superiority of the Commons. Our suggested package would mean that the Commons was pre-eminent as the only wholly elected House (with a voting system based on individual constituencies which made it more representative by being closer to the voters); strengthened in relation to Lords' powers, and reinforced as the sole source of government authority. Far from threatening the Commons, a stronger second chamber with clearly defined functions could help the primary chamber in its job. Chapter Five suggests criteria for sustaining the right balance between the two Houses.

23. The Royal Commission, Government and Parliament all need to show vision. The Joint Committee of MPs and peers which is to follow the Royal Commission will also have a responsibility to produce, or at least not frustrate, an outcome which strengthens Parliament as a whole.

24. In the transition to a fully reformed House, the White Paper's principle of parity between the two main parties as to life peers should be continued while phasing-in the reformed house, in order that the results of elections are reflected in the political balance.

25. The real choice is whether we come down on the side of better governance or the side of the relative ease which the present system gives to the executive.

NOTES AND REFERENCES

Introduction

1. 'Modernising Parliament: Reforming the House of Lords', January 1999, Cm 4183 (Chapter 3, paragraph 2)
2. See pages 33–5
3. Lords Hansard, 14 October 1998, col 925
4. *Today* programme, BBC Radio 4, 30 July 1998, reported in *The Times*, 31 July 1998; also *Guardian*, 6 November 1998
5. See the *Independent*, 28 September 1998, *The Times*, 26 October 1998
6. *Newsnight*, BBC2, 2 December 1998
7. *The Times*, 4 December 1998

Chapter One

1. Lords Hansard, 11 June 1984, col 898
2. See Chapter Two for the use of the Parliament Acts in the European Parliamentary Elections Bill 1998
3. These and following figures are based, except where stated otherwise, on the annual and sessional statistics of the business of the House 1993–7, compiled by the House of Lords Information Office
4. 'Private' bills, by contrast, concern the rights or interests of private individuals or bodies where legislation is necessary to change or regulate those interests. 'Hybrid' bills,

which also fall outside the Acts, are public bills which affect private rights (such as legislation authorising the Channel Tunnel rail link)

5. An amendment to the motion for second reading expressing a reason why the bill is considered unsatisfactory
6. Lords Hansard, 16 August 1945
7. Lord Carrington, 'Reflect on Things Past: The Memoirs of Lord Carrington' (1988), pp 77–8, quoted in 'The Salisbury Doctrine', House of Lords Library Note, 97/004
8. Lords Hansard, 15 October 1998, col 1162. See also Viscount Cranborne, Politeia Anniversary Lecture, 4 December 1996

Chapter Two

1. Lords Hansard, 14 October 1998, col 977
2. White Paper, Chapter 5, paragraph 5
3. Conference: 'Labour and the House of Lords', 8 June 1998, col 76
4. Labour Party figures
5. Lords Hansard, 15 October 1998, col 1066
6. D. Shell and D. Beamish (eds), *The House of Lords at Work*, OUP, 1993, quoted in PLP fact sheet on the House of Lords, September 1997
7. Figures from House of Lords Information Office
8. Research by Opposition Whips' Office, 1996
9. Figures quotes by Baroness Jay of Paddington, Lords Hansard, 14 October 1998, col 923, from a survey by Nicholas Baldwin, quoted in D. Shell and D. Beamish (eds), *The House of Lords at Work*, OUP, Oxford, 1993
10. Initial report of Constitutional Commission (the Mackay Commission), September 1998, Appendix 1
11. *Daily Mail*, 5 November 1998
12. Lady Saltoun, Lords Hansard Debs 14 October 1998, col 1019
13. 'The Athenian Option: Radical Reform of the House of Lords', Demos, June 1998
14. See debate on Lords reform, Lords Hansard, 14 & 15 October 1998

15. *Daily Telegraph*, 23 October 1998
16. 'Enhancing Our Democracy: Reforming the House of Lords', Tory Reform Group, June 1998
17. Conference: 'Labour and the House of Lords', 8 June 1998, col 76
18. Lords Hansard, 15 October 1998, col 1028
19. Lecture to the think tank Politeia, 1 April 1998
20. Exchange with Lord Rodgers, Lords Hansard, 14 October 1998, col 933
21. Quoted in D. Butler, A. Adonis and T. Travers, *Failure in British Government: The Politics of the Poll Tax*, OUP, 1994.
22. The then record being 509 votes on a motion on entry to the EEC on 28 October 1971. This was surpassed in 1993 in a vote on the Maastricht Treaty, when the Major Government defeated a call by Lady Thatcher for a referendum by an enormous 445 votes to 176
23. Lords Hansard, 18 November 1998, col 1361
24. Lords Hansard, 13 March 1980, col 1220
25. Education (Schools) Bill 1992, 2 March 1992
26. Donald Shell includes a detailed account in his *The House of Lords*, Phillip Allan, 1988 (2nd edition, Harvester Wheatsheaf, 1992)

Chapter Three

1. 'Modernising Parliament: Reforming the House of Lords', January 1999, Cm 4183
2. Lords Hansard, 20 January 1999, col 593
3. Chapter 2, paragraph 24
4. Chapter 1, paragraph 24
5. *Financial Times*, 22 January 1999
6. Chapter 2, paragraph 26
7. E.g., *The Times, Daily Telegraph*, 21 January 1999
8. Chapter 5, paragraph 11
9. *Financial Times*, 22 January 1999
10. Chapter 3, paragraph 8
11. Chapter 5, paragraph 11
12. Chapter 6, paragraph 5

13. Excludes Lord Longford as a hereditary peer of first creation
14. Chapter 2, paragraph 8; Chapter 3, paragraph 8 and following
15. 'An Appointed Upper House: Lessons from Canada', Meg Russell, Constitution Unit, November 1998
16. See also speech by Lord Cooke of Thorndon, Lords Hansard, 15 October 1998, col 1130
17. Chapter 8, paragraph 22
18. Chapter 7, paragraph 7
19. Chapter 7, paragraph 9
20. Chapter 7, paragraph 13
21. Lords Hansard, 20 January 1999, col 594
22. Chapter 8, paragraph 5
23. Chapter 8, paragraph 4
24. Chapter 8, paragraph 6
25. Chapter 8, paragraph 8
26. Chapter 8, paragraph 23
27. Chapter 8, paragraph 27
28. Chapter 8, paragraph 28
29. Chapter 8, paragraph 33
30. Chapter 8, paragraph 35
31. Chapter 8, paragraph 35
32. *Guardian*, 6 November 1998. The report was not directly linked to a specific model
33. *Guardian*, 9 December 1998
34. A similar proportion of the 43 per cent supported this option in the Joseph Rowntree Trust and MORI State of the Nation Survey, May 1995

Chapter Four

1. See 'Rebalancing the Lords: The Numbers', Constitution Unit, January 1998
2. Interview in *The Times*, 29 December 1998
3. Yorks NUM, Committee of Privileges, 1975
4. 'An Appointed Upper House: Lessons from Canada', Meg Russell, Constitution Unit, November 1998
5. *The Times*, 29 December 1998

6. 'Modern Local Government: In Touch with the People', July 1998, Cm 4014
7. See report of letter to MPs from Dick Caborn MP, Minister of State, DETR, *Guardian*, 2 January 1998
8. Announced by the Leader of the House of Commons, Margaret Beckett, on 14 January 1999
9. 'Modern Local Government: In Touch with the People', July 1998, Cm 4014, Chapter 4
10. J. Mitchell and A. Davies, 'Reforming the Lords', IPPR, June 1993
11. Plant Committee, Appendix 2
12. It was also proposed in a discussion paper, 'Straight to the Senate', Katharine Quarmby, IPPR, April 1998
13. Interview, *The Times*, 29 December 1998
14. Labour's position is in its 1997 manifesto. For the Conservative stance, see the announcement by William Hague, 13 July 1998 (Initial Report of the Constitutional Commission, Appendix 1). The Liberal Democrats' policy is in 'Moving Ahead: Towards a Citizens' Britain' (1998), section 3.3

Chapter Five

1. Reform of the House of Lords Bill, Graham Allen MP, 1988/9
2. 1998 Policy Paper ('Moving Ahead: Towards a Citizens' Britain')
3. Lord Hailsham called in 1976 for a House elected by regional PR, and in 1983 an unofficial Conservative study recommended an elected House
4. Disraeli Lecture, *Independent* and *Guardian*, 30 October 1998
5. Lords Hansard, 14 October 1998, cols 944, 976/7
6. Another recent study has proposed a two-tier chamber of voting and non-voting peers, with two-thirds of the 420 voting peers being elected by STV and one-third appointed: 'Peers in Parliament Reformed', William Wyndham, 1998
7. *Random Recollections of the House of Lords,* by the

author of *Random Collections of the House of Commons*, i.e., James Grant, London, 1836

8. 'Making the Law', November 1992
9. See recommendations 44, 49–50 and 71
10. In proposing the greater use of what it called 'first reading committees', the Hansard Society Commission was thinking primarily of the House of Commons. There would seem to be no reason, however, why such committees should not be introduced in the second chamber
11. 'Human Rights Legislation', Constitution Unit, November 1996

BIBLIOGRAPHY

Butler, David, Adonis, Andrew and Travers, Tony, *Failure in British Government: The Politics of the Poll Tax*, Oxford University Press, 1994

Dickson, Bruce and Carmichael, Paul (eds), *The House of Lords: Its Parliamentary and Judicial Roles*, Hart Publishing, 1999

Grant, James, *Random Recollections of the House of Lords, from the year 1830 to 1836 . . .* By the author of 'Random Recollections of the House of Commons', Smith, Elder and Co, 1836

Mitchell, Jeremy and Davies, Anne, *Reforming the Lords*, Institute for Public Policy Research, 1993

Morgan, Janet P., *The House of Lords and the Labour Government, 1964–70*, Oxford University Press, 1975

Shell, Donald, *The House of Lords*, Philip Allan, 1998 (second edition, Harvester Wheatsheaf, 1992)

Smith, E.A., *The House of Lords in British Politics and Society 1815–1911*, Longman, 1992

Charter 88, 'Reform of the House of Lords', Policy paper, September 1998

Conservative Central Office, *The House of Lords. The Report of the Conservative Review Committee* (The Home Report), March 1978

Constitutional Commission to consider options for the Second Chamber (the Mackay Commission), *Initial Report of the Constitutional Commission*, September 1998

Constitution Unit, The, *Reform of the House of Lords*, 1996

Constitution Unit, The, *An Appointed Upper House: Lessons from Canada*, Meg Russell, November 1998

Constitution Unit, The, *Checks and Balances in Single Chamber Parliaments: A Comparative Study* (February and September 1998)

Constitution Unit, The, *Human Rights Legislation*, Briefing, November 1996

Constitution Unit, The, *Rebalancing the Lords: The Numbers*, January 1998

Cranborne, Viscount, 'The End of the Era of Representative Democracy?', Speech to Politeia, 1 April 1998

Demos, *The Athenian Option. Radical Reform for the House of Lords*, Anthony Barnett and Peter Carty, June 1998

Hansard Society for Parliamentary Government, The, *Making the Law: Report of the Hansard Commission on the Legislative Process*, November 1992

Institute for Constitutional Research, 'Labour and the House of Lords', Conference Proceedings, June 1998

Kent, Nicholas, 'Enhancing our Democracy: Reforming the House of Lords', Tory Reform Group, June 1998

Labour Party, The, *Time to Get Britain Working Again*, Manifesto for the General Election, 1992

Labour Party, The, *Report of the Working Party on Electoral Systems* (The Plant Report), 1993

Labour Party, The, The John Smith Memorial Lecture, given by the Rt Hon Tony Blair MP, 7 February 1996

Labour Party, The/Liberal Democrats, The, *Report of the Joint Consultative Committee on Constitutional Reform* (The Cook/Maclennan Report), March 1997

Liberal Democrats, The, *Moving Ahead: Towards a Citizens' Britain*, Policy Paper, 1998

Osmond, John, *Reforming the Lords and Changing Britain*, Fabian Society, August 1998

Power, Greg, 'Representatives of the People? The Constituency Role of MPs', Fabian Society, October 1998

Quarmby, Katherine, 'Straight to the Senate', IPPR Discussion Paper, April 1998

Welfare, Damien, 'An Anachronism with Relevance: The Revival of the House of Lords in the 1980s and its Defence of Local Government', *Parliamentary Affairs*, April 1992

Official papers

Conference on the Reform of the Second Chamber, Letter from Viscount Bryce to the Prime Minister (The Bryce Report), Cmnd 9038, 1918 (reprinted 1955)
House of Lords Reform, Cmnd 3799, Noveber 1968
Modern Local Government. In touch with the People, Cm 4014, July 1998
Modernising Parliament. Reforming the House of Lords, Cm 4183, January 1999
Parliament Bill. Agreed Statement on Conclusion of Conference of Party Leaders, February–April, 1948
Report of the Independent Commission on the Voting System The, (The Jenkins Report), Cm 4090–1, October 1998
Scotland's Parliament, Cm 3658, July 1997
Voice for Wales, A, Cm 3718, July 1997

Parliamentary publications

Annual Report and Accounts, House of Lords, 1997–98
Government of Wales Act 1998
House of Lords Bill, House of Commons, Bill 34, 19 January 1999
House of Lords Briefing Papers on:
  Analysis of Composition (4 January 1999)
  Scrutinising the Executive – The Delegated Powers and Deregulation Committee (December 1997)
  The Work of the House of Lords – Its Role, Functions and Powers (October 1998)
  The Financing of the House of Lords (October 1998)
  Bills and How They Become Law (June 1997)
  History of the House of Lords (May 1997)
  The Judicial Work of the House of Lords (December 1997)
  Scrutinising European Legislation – The European Communities Committee (October 1997)

House of Lords Reform: Developments since the General Election, Barry K Winetrobe, House of Commons Library, Research Paper 98/85, August 1998

Proposals for Reform of the Composition and Powers of the House of Lords, 1968–98, House of Lords Library Note, 98/004, July 1998

Salisbury Doctrine, The, House of Lords Library, Library Note 97/004

Scotland Act 1998

INDEX

216